Judge Sam King

A Memoir

JUDGE SAM KING
A Memoir

❧

by Samuel P. King

with Jerry Burris and Ken Kobayashi

WATERMARK
PUBLISHING

iv

ISBN 978-1-935690-38-2

Library of Congress Control Number: 2013939242

Photo credits
pp. ii, 27-29, 32-34, 88 bottom, 89-90: courtesy the King family
pp. 30-31, 84-87, 88 top: courtesy the *Honolulu Star-Advertiser*
p. 33 bottom: Mike Tsukamoto, *Honolulu Star-Bulletin*
p. 88 bottom, 90: Salvatore S. Lanzilotti

Design and production
Leo Gonzalez
Angela Wu-Ki

Watermark Publishing
1000 Bishop St., Suite 806
Honolulu, HI 96813
Telephone 1-808-587-7766
Toll-free 1-866-900-BOOK
sales@bookshawaii.net
www.bookshawaii.net

Printed in Korea

CONTENTS

Foreword

Judge Samuel Pailthorpe King was a member of one of the most illustrious families in the history of Hawai'i. I had the high privilege of working with his father, Samuel Wilder King, when he was governor of the Territory of Hawai'i.

Samuel Wilder King was a very dedicated public servant. While we had disagreements on policy issues, I don't believe we ever used harsh rhetoric during our relationship. His wife, Pauline Nāwahineokala'i Evans, the first lady of Hawai'i and Sam's mother, was an extraordinary woman. Full of grace and charm, she was the perfect first lady for that period of our history. I was so impressed by her demeanor and commitment to society. When I was called upon to participate in the christening of the first U.S. naval vessel named after the state of Hawai'i, I submitted Mrs. King's name as sponsor of this submarine. At the time, it was a member of the world's largest and most powerful class of submarines.

Judge King and I had our differences, particularly when we were a bit younger. In those youthful days, when he was involved in the political events of the 1950s, he was expected to play a major role. After all, he was the son of the governor. We had a few contentious exchanges. Shortly after that, the Democrats swept into power in territorial Hawai'i.

A few years later, when Sam King's name was submitted for a federal judgeship, I did not hesitate. I supported the nomination. And history shows he served on the bench in an honorable and deliberative fashion. There were times when he expressed himself rather dramatically; he always got his point across. It was clear to all who dealt with him that he was sincere. He was the real deal. Hawai'i was fortunate to have had Sam King on the bench. He served the people of Hawai'i well and brought honor to our state and nation.

— U.S. Senator Daniel K. Inouye

INTRODUCTION

Samuel P. King saw Hawai'i through a century of profound transformation. Born in China in 1916, King was raised in Territorial-era Hawai'i. He was on the island of O'ahu during the bombing of Pearl Harbor and was present in Japan days after the bombing of Hiroshima. As the chairman of Hawai'i's Republican Party in 1954, he witnessed Hawai'i's Democratic Revolution firsthand, and, in 1959, he celebrated the statehood that his father, a former Territorial governor, had fought hard to secure. King presided over a state and then a federal courtroom for more than 50 years, deciding cases that made local and national headlines. In the process, he was not only a witness to history, he helped shape Hawai'i's history and future.

King's Hawaiian roots span eras. He was the son of a part-Hawaiian governor of the Territory of Hawai'i, the grandson of the minister of the interior of the Republic of Hawai'i and the great-grandson of a Supreme Court justice of the Kingdom of Hawai'i. His great-great-grandparents were an O'ahu *ali'i* and a *haole* governor of O'ahu appointed by Kamehameha I in the 1790s.

King had all the impressive trappings of a federal judge—the JD from Yale, the baritone voice, the black robe, the highest seat in the courtroom, bailiffs and clerks doing his bidding. Yet what people noticed about him was that he genuinely cared about everybody. King acknowledged everyone he met, from civic and business leaders to clerks, waiters and janitors. He even visited convicts he had sentenced to prison.

King didn't care much about material wealth. For decades, while serving as a federal judge, he parked his 1968 Volkswagen bug next to the Jaguars and Cadillacs in the judges' parking area. When his wife, Anne, suggested that he change to an automatic shift, he bought an old station wagon with a window that wouldn't close.

It would be hard to think of another public figure in Hawai'i who had more fun than Sam King. He was well known in the community for his sense of humor and irreverence. He was particularly fond of calling the members of the United States Supreme Court "the guys in the black muʻumuʻus." Every day was an adventure for King, and, if the day didn't provide an occasion to laugh, he would find a way to make one.

One day, when King was presiding over the state's family court, a woman testified to a dozen good reasons she should be granted a divorce from her no-good husband—and it seemed as though she were just getting started. King kindly said, "Madam, I can give you only one divorce."

What King was deadly serious about was protecting people, particularly those who had little or no power of their own. King presided over some of the most sensational of the organized-crime trials in the 1970s and upheld the 1967 Hawaiʻi Land Reform Act that shifted property ownership in Hawaiʻi from large trusts to ordinary citizens. He liked to observe that "people aren't created for laws; laws are created for people." He also commented that the whole purpose of government, besides keeping its people safe, is to protect the under-privileged from the privileged.

In his eighties, King, along with four other community leaders, spearheaded the "Broken Trust" effort that contributed to the ousting of Bishop Estate trustees and reform of the estate's operating rules. He knew that his participation would itself be highly controversial, but that did not stop him. During that tumultuous time, King told a reporter, "Every judge has an obligation: If you see something wrong in the community, you speak out against it."

The loves of King's life were his family, his work, his books (his personal library numbered over 6,000 volumes) and his homeland. When he passed away in December 2010, Governor Neil Abercrombie called him "the heart and soul of Hawaiʻi."

In 2009, longtime courts and legal reporter Ken Kobayashi and veteran political reporter Jerry Burris began a series of recorded conversations with King. For months, they met several times a week in the judge's book-lined, fourth-floor office at the Prince Kūhiō Federal Building, with a magnificent view of Honolulu Harbor. King, with his sister Pauline, had helped name the building's four original courtrooms: ʻAha Kanawai (Place of Law), ʻAha Kūpono (Place of Justice), ʻAha Kaulike (A Place of Equity) and ʻAha Nonoi (Place of Appeal). With nearly a century to cover—he was 93 at the time, and still working—there was a lot to talk about.

This memoir was based on those conversations, on an excellent oral history conducted by King's former law clerk, Susan Lee Waggener, and on the vast trove of writing, news stories, speeches and other material carefully saved and organized by Anne King and by his longtime secretary, Rebecca Berry. In addition, Anne King and Anne and Sam's daughters—Charlotte King Stretch and Louise King Lanzilotti—were instrumental in helping edit this memoir.

—*Jerry Burris and Ken Kobayashi*

Chapter One

NAPPY AND FRIENDS: THE HEYDAY OF ORGANIZED CRIME

My place of work at the start of my career as a federal judge was in the old Federal Courthouse, next to the main Post Office in downtown Honolulu. From the front steps of that building you could look across King Street—not named after my family; there's a Queen Street, too, you know—to 'Iolani Palace, where my father had served as governor.

I still remember the day I climbed up to my place at the bench in that building and saw these five local boys standing before me. *They look like the front line of the Los Angeles Rams*, I thought to myself. They might have looked like professional football players at first glance, but there was something else: a coldness in their eyes that could give you chills. There was one particular guy who you knew you were going to be afraid of even before you saw him. He would just walk around and you would say: "Oh, boy, I'd better stay out of his way."

The five were Wilfred "Nappy" Pulawa, Alema Leota, Henry Huihui, Alvin Kaohu and Robert "Bobby" Wilson. Pulawa was the reputed underworld leader in Hawai'i. I didn't know much about these guys at the time but learned during their trial—for conspiracy to avoid federal taxes—that they were at the heart of a criminal syndicate, or "mob," as some of the media called it. Nappy Pulawa was the leader, and not just of this crew.

I never understood why people would say there was no organized crime in Honolulu. Of course there was! Generally, organized crime centered on gambling. There was a little bit of this, "You pay us so much a month or we come in and destroy you"— the protection racket. There was some prostitution and drugs, but gambling was the big one. The thing about organized crime is that it would not be possible without the people who break the law because they want to gamble and hire prostitutes. They think they can out-maneuver the police.

At the time there were two different groups running gambling, but then the Samoans came in and kind of took it over. The expert on the subject was Larry Mehau, a former police officer and Big Island rancher who ran a security company. He was also occasionally described as the "Godfather" of

Organized Crime in Hawai'i, a charge he always denied. He was influential—big in Democratic politics, working with people like Jack Burns and George Ariyoshi. I think he also helped my Republican friend Pat Saiki when she ran for governor.

Mehau knew all the boys who were in and out of trouble. In fact, he used to hire them when they got out of prison. Some were pretty cold-blooded, but Mehau said he felt they deserved a second chance.

In 1977, the word "Godfather" appeared in a Maui newspaper, the *Valley Isle*, in an article that implicated Mehau in the deaths of several people. The word was picked up and published elsewhere, so Mehau sued for defamation, not just the *Valley Isle* but most of the local TV stations, newspapers and radio news stations. The case was first assigned to Judge James Burns, Governor John Burns' son, but Judge Burns stepped aside because he was a personal friend of Mehau's. Burns was not alone; nine of the 13 circuit court judges also declined to hear the case. The remaining four were not asked because they were about to retire or were otherwise unavailable. The case was settled out of court.

It made for quite a circus in the news, but I was watching from the sidelines because it was a state matter and I was at the time a federal judge.

People used to ask me: "Was Mehau the Godfather?" I really can't say. I met with Mehau only once, long after these trials occurred, and I never had him in my court. My position has always been that no one is a crook unless so proven.

The existence of organized crime in Hawai'i is another matter, and it wasn't just the trials that lead me to conclude that there was. I had access to police transcripts, wiretaps, that kind of thing. In those days, if witnesses started to cooperate with law enforcement, they sometimes disappeared.

While I learned a lot during the trials, there was also coverage in the newspapers that helped flesh out who the bad guys were and what they were capable of. Some of the best was by *Honolulu Advertiser* reporter Gene Hunter, whose 1970 series on organized crime earned him a nomination for the Pulitzer Prize.

Hunter described loose coalitions of local figures who warred with each other and at times with outside groups that sought to get into the local underground businesses, particularly gambling, hard drugs and prostitution. These were far from the lovable boobs in Damon Runyon's "Guys and Dolls" stories; they were hardcore characters who knew what they wanted and were not afraid to do what they had to do to get it. Still, most of them were local boys with links to the community and friends and family who had nothing to do with the criminal activities. I couldn't help thinking about that. Some of the worst of them had relatives who worked in the school system, for the city and state—even the newspapers!

While organized crime covered the whole state, it was mostly on Oʻahu because of tourism. People come here as guests, and they want gambling, they want a girl—a Hawaiian. Someone had to organize that. But in some ways we were fortunate. There was relative peace in those days because when a guy like Pulawa was in charge, anybody who stepped out of line wasn't around very long. Also, because the main figures were local, lots of people were able to check up on them and help the police. I have a feeling that's changed now. It's not run by local boys anymore.

A lot of people say, "What's wrong with a little gambling?" Perfectly nice people go from Hawaiʻi to Las Vegas all the time to gamble. My secretary, Rebecca Berry, was one of them. In fact, she eventually won more than a million bucks from a slot machine in Minnesota while visiting her daughter.

But where gambling is illegal, as it is here, the gambling profits go to finance other illegal activities. That's the problem.

When Pulawa and the others rose to power in the local syndicate, their group was focused on gambling, but they quickly developed an organization so sophisticated and organized that, as Hunter put it in 1970, "it may well be ready for takeover by the Mafia."

By the time they got before me in 1974, some of the rough edges had been sanded off. They were cleaned up, polite and fairly well spoken. But that look in their eyes was something else.

People always ask me if these guys intimidated me, and the truth is they did not. In a sense, you could say they were professionals. They did not resent what I had to do. The judge has his role and they have theirs. But there was at least one time where a threat against a witness appeared serious.

One day we got a call that they were planning to kill a witness right in court as he was testifying, so I told my law clerk, "We gotta get more security." We soon received help from the Mainland, including a woman who was a U.S. Marshal. She was the sweetest thing that you ever saw, but in her little purse was a handgun. Defense lawyers complained about all the security people standing around with earphones in their ears, but they didn't notice the one with the little purse.

The Pulawa trial ended in a guilty verdict. I remember that night well. While the marshals saw that all the jurors got home safely, I went down to the courthouse parking lot, got into my Volkswagen bug and headed home, alone. When I got to my house my wife told me the marshals had just called, saying that there might be a threat on my life. Some guy had been overheard in a bar somewhere, saying he was going to "get King."

I wasn't too concerned about my safety. I remember telling the marshals: "Oh no, they're not interested in me. If anything, look out for the witnesses." In fact, I was then and am still today listed in the phone book. You know, if you shoot a judge, another one will just come in. If the bad guys are going to intimidate or threaten anyone, it will be witnesses or perhaps the jury. The most dangerous cases for a judge aren't criminal trials but family relations, where things get taken personally.

I would say that my juries were pretty brave. They would have seen the Hollywood movies where there's some member of the jury who gets a note that his wife and small child have been detained in Nebraska or something and won't be returned until the case is over. Nothing like that ever happened in my court as far as I know, but it must have been on some of the jurors' minds. In fact, there was a case in which some criminals broke into the home of a Waikīkī jewelry-store owner and held his wife and kids captive. If he didn't turn over the goods, they threatened to harm his family. Some might have remembered that.

There were actually two federal trials for Pulawa. The first was for conspiracy. The feds alleged that Pulawa and his enforcers had conspired to cheat the federal government out of taxes owed. The Internal Revenue Service had the goods on Pulawa, but cheating the government out of taxes is a very esoteric charge. Adding all the other defendants into it as a conspiracy weakened the case. It turned out to be a stupid charge. It also led to one of the best bits of lawyering I had ever seen. At the perfect time in the middle of the trial, local defense counsel Brook Hart pointed to the defendants and asked the jury if they truly believed that these five characters were capable of getting together and saying, "Hey, let's cheat the United States out of Pulawa's taxes."

Boom! Acquitted.

In the Pulawa conspiracy case, while the lawyering was good, it added up to only a small victory. Those five walked out of the courthouse smiling, but within hours their car was pulled over and they were re-arrested. This time, the feds got smart and charged Pulawa alone for income tax evasion. So the next time around, he wasn't so lucky.

For all his reputation for violence, Pulawa was remarkably mild and soft-spoken during each of his trials. In fact, I often had to tell him to speak up so that the jury could hear him. He claimed he was a small guy in the operation, collecting money and running errands, and that all his money and other assets came from his wife. Pulawa's wife testified that properties she and her husband owned in California, as well as large amounts of money accumulated in savings accounts, were from her $400-a-month job as a drugstore clerk. I'm not sure the jury bought that. One witness, Clarence Handa, who was known as a gambling operator, testified at trial that he was approached by Pulawa over beers in 1970 and was told he had to cough up $20,000 in protection money. Eventually, they settled at a payment of $200 a week. Handa said: "He tells me, if I don't pay, 'I bump you off or you get off this island.'"

After the jury found Pulawa guilty, I sentenced him to 24 years in prison, which at the time was the longest federal tax-evasion sentence in recorded history. I suppose he can take some pride in knowing he got more time than famous mobsters such as Al Capone and Mickey Cohen, who got eleven and fifteen years for similar crimes.

I have a strong philosophy that prison is not the right place for most people, even guilty people. But it does seem to me that if ever there was a case for applying the maximum term possible, that was it.

The judge in a jury case normally keeps his or her opinions to himself, but federal rules allow comment on trial testimony. I had no problem doing so in this case after the trial was over. "I see no other verdict you could have reached in this matter," I told the jurors before they were dismissed.

I sometimes gave tough sentences, but I always thought about the impact of prison on the person and his family. And I made it a point to visit people I had sentenced, even on the West Coast, where many were sent. I felt I had a responsibility to do that. I'd check in with them, see if they were eating right, if they were getting their rice, that kind of thing.

I will never forget one visit to Lompoc federal prison, when I was in California for some kind of trial. Even though I was a judge, I had to check in with the warden and go through security and so forth. I told them, "I'm here to see my boys and girls."

They had an outdoor recreation yard and there I was on a bench with Pulawa on one side and "Thunder" Park on the other (her first name was Yvonne, but everyone called her Thunder). A very big girl, and kind of interesting. She had some criminal activities but she was also an artist and an activist for low-income people. It was a beautiful day, California weather. They left us alone, but I knew the guards were watching. Thunder kept saying "Judge, you gotta get me out of here." I told her if she'd lose some weight, I would see what I could do, but nothing came of that. Pulawa kept telling me "Judge, sending me here was the best thing that could have happened to me." But I didn't believe it. As far as I was concerned, it was just *hoʻomalimali*.

With Pulawa out of the way for the time being, government officials suspected someone else would step up to take his place. The most likely suspect was Earl K.H. Kim. By the mid-1970s, federal authorities were very interested in Kim, also known as "the Old Man." They suspected him of running a statewide bookmaking operation. FBI agents were keeping a close eye on Kim, even when he was in a friend's apartment. They set up a surveillance system using an 800-mm telescope to watch Kim from a quarter-mile away. It went both ways, because Kim would sometimes pull out binoculars to see if anyone was spying on him. The telescope must have beaten the binoculars, because the feds spotted Kim meeting with other associates in the gambling case. They even saw him reading a sports journal! These observations led to a wiretap, which led to gambling charges for Kim.

In the case that came before me, I ruled the evidence obtained by telescope was inadmissible. I said that authorities have an interest in keeping an eye on the bad guys, but there are limits to what they can do, and their evidence is admissible only so long as what they saw was visible to any passerby. What they saw through a telescope in this case did not satisfy that test. The government put up a good fight, though. They noted the newspapers were reporting that more and more people were using telescopes to peek into high-rise apartments and condominiums in Honolulu, and that Kim should have known this was the case; therefore he "knowingly exposed" his activities to public viewing. I had to shake my head. "The fact that Peeping Toms abound does not license the government to follow suit," I wrote. When I suppressed any evidence obtained from the telescope peeping, it was the first federal ruling on that point. I believe it is still cited as good law across the country.

As for spying on people, I think law enforcement still uses a telescope for a look-see from time to time. They just don't tell us about it.

Funny thing about Kim—he was a smart guy, and he was kind of a family man, father of two and so forth. The rest of Kim's family was terrific. One worked for the City & County of Honolulu, and another might have been a lawyer. They were all nice people. Earl just went off the tracks. But unlike Pulawa and some of the others, he didn't seem like a violent person. It started with just gambling, but it slipped over into other things. If a customer wanted a girl, or some drugs or something, he would be only too happy to oblige, according to the information provided to me.

I don't know how he maintained discipline in his organization. He didn't look like the strong-arm type, but you couldn't help but notice that when people ran afoul of his guys, they somehow either disappeared or were found dead.

After Kim was convicted and sentenced, on top of ten years he had remaining from previous convictions for gun violations and smuggling marijuana in California, he said to me: "Judge, I just can't stop gambling. You have to send me to Las Vegas." What he meant was that, once he was released or if he could get probation, he would already be in Las Vegas and could get a job as a waiter or busboy and gamble legally. He repeated over and over, "I can't stop," and I knew that to be true. In fact, in open court I acknowledged that there was little hope his time in prison would cure him of his gambling addiction. I told him, "I wouldn't be surprised if you ended up running a gambling operation in prison."

Kim was a character. He thanked me for placing him in confinement pending his trial, saying it gave him time to read. In fact, I remember that he brought a *Time* magazine article to court one day; it was about the argument for legalized gambling.

These were some of the last major organized-crime cases we had in Hawai'i. While they generated a lot of publicity, there would be many other high-profile cases to come during my years on the bench. But before I talk about those, allow me a few words about how it all began. Hawai'i's courtrooms are a long way from the shores of the Yangtze River, and how I got from one to the other is an important part of the story. ❧

Chapter Two

Born in China, Roots Deep in Hawai'i

In 1916, the year I was born, Europe was fighting what was said to be the war that would end all wars. Hawai'i had been a U.S. territory for just 15 years. Sugar and pineapple fields covered Ō'ahu's 'Ewa and central plains. And Honolulu was more of a town than a city. It started in Kalihi and ended in Kaimukī. Waikīkī had only a couple of hotels.

My siblings were born in Hawai'i, but, by chance, I was born in China.

My father was stationed there as a U.S. Navy gunboat captain. Some of the officers' wives went back to Hawai'i to give birth so their children would be born on American soil. My mother did that with my older sister, Charlotte. They traveled by ship in those days—no jet planes. But when my turn came around, mother decided it would be easier to give birth in Hankow. I came into the world with the help of a shipboard doctor in an English boardinghouse in Hankow's Russian concession. I was born with a caul, which some people believe is a sign of good luck. I don't know whether that is true, but I found through my life that many things came easy to me.

China was a rugged place in those days. There was danger, but, in many ways, life was pretty good for those stationed in far-off China. My parents remembered cocktail parties, tennis games and "twisting the tiger's tail," which meant to go gamble in the local town. China stayed out of World War I, but it was an unstable place. The emperor had just been deposed, and warring factions were fighting for control.

Most of the Western powers thought it would be best to station some military might in China to protect their various interests. Russia, Great Britain, France and the U.S. all set up quarters in the town of Hankow (now called Wuhan), about 1,000 kilometers up the Yangtze River from Shanghai. They used it as a base for their fleets patrolling the Yangtze.

My dad was a good river pilot. He had to be. When the Yangtze overflowed its banks, you didn't know where you were. Unless you were a qualified navigator, you might find yourself high and dry in the middle of a rice paddy. Dad received a commendation from the Navy for the excellent condition of his vessel, the USS *Samar*, and his crew of forty or so. In Kemp Tolley's book

Yangtze Patrol, published after my dad left China, the *Samar* makes an appearance as a boat with a reputation for the high quality of its mess—the food laid out for the crew. Most of the ships carried a well-stocked liquor cabinet to entertain visiting dignitaries, and I expect the *Samar* was no exception.

While the Chinese crew labored below decks, the officers would sit on wicker chairs on the deck and survey the passing scene, Tolley wrote. He quotes a skipper, who might have been my dad, as saying the *Samar* had a storage problem: When coal or other heavy goods were brought on board, they produced a distinctive list. This created a crablike quality to the *Samar's* movement along the Yangtze. "We frequently sidled up and down the river, much to the amusement of British gunboat sailors, whose ships were much more modern," one skipper recalled in Tolley's book.

My father's duties were varied. They included protecting American interests, which at the time were mainly missionaries and some commercial holdings. One of his most memorable trips, though, was a rescue mission to pick up Yuan Shikai, who had become the leader of one of the warring Chinese factions after the empress was deposed, and get him to Shanghai alive. There had been some kind of scandal, and Yuan took refuge in my father's gunboat, along with his mistress and a bag of gold. Along the way, the *Samar* came under fire from the shore. No harm. Later, my dad would say he didn't think they were truly interested in hitting anyone; they just wanted to show that the scoundrel was not welcome to return.

I don't have any memories of China, but there is a photo of me in the arms of my Chinese *amah*. I'm often asked if I can speak Chinese, a tone language. I tell them I learned to cry in Chinese. Other babies go "waaah." But, in Chinese, I go "wa-aah." Even today, on top of the riverbank where once stood the boardinghouse I was born in, there is a stele with all kinds of Chinese writing on it. I tell everybody it says, "Sam King was born here."

My dad got his sea legs from his father, who was port captain for the Wilder Steamship Company. Samuel Gardner Wilder was good to my grandfather and my father was named after him. A lot of people think the Kings must be related to the Wilders, but there's no blood relation.

When Hawai'i's provisional government was put together, Wilder was asked to serve as minister of the interior. "No," he said, "give it to Captain King." My grandfather served in that position until he died. There's a picture of him, sitting there with President Sanford Dole, the minister of foreign relations and the attorney general.

My grandfather had set sail from Donegal when he was fourteen. He eventually ended up in Hawai'i and married my grandmother, Charlotte Davis, whose Hawaiian ancestors were from O'ahu. The first non-Hawaiian on her side of the family, Oliver Holmes, came to Hawai'i in 1793, a generation before the missionaries got here. Holmes left a ship that had departed out of Plymouth, Massachusetts, to stay in Hawai'i. As he wrote in a letter that is in the State Archives, he wanted to "tarry a while in these lovely isles."

At the time, King Kamehameha was offering all kinds of inducements to knowledgeable haoles who could fire cannons. That's how he conquered the islands. Kamehameha handed Holmes a job governing O'ahu, and a wife—a Hawaiian *ali'i* named Mahi—whose father, Kaliniho'oulumokuikekai, had been pushed over the Pali by Kamehameha.

I could never verify whether I was related to Oliver Wendell Holmes, Jr., the respected associate justice on the U.S. Supreme Court. An ancestor of mine who was the grandson of Oliver Holmes, William Heath Davis, wrote a book, *60 Years in California*, in which he says our Oliver Holmes was named after either the jurist or the jurist's father. It would be nice if we could prove that connection. I always admired the philosophy of Justice Oliver Wendell Holmes, Jr. He moved the law away from formalism, toward realism. He once wrote: "The life of the law has not been logic, it has been experience." Over my years on the bench, I have surely come to agree with that.

My father had a great influence on me, both in my personal life and in my judicial outlook. In an odd way, he even influenced my religious orientation and my life path. I might have graduated from that good Catholic institution, St. Louis High School, instead of Punahou, if it weren't for a duck.

When my father attended school at St. Louis, every morning started off with chapel. One day, as my father was walking to the chapel, he saw a lame duck on the side of the road. He picked it up and put it in his shirt. The poor little thing was quiet, for a while. But after a few minutes in chapel, the duck started to quack. The St. Louis Brothers didn't stand for any nonsense, so my father got suspended for a week. That made my grandfather so mad he pulled his sons, all five of them, out of the school.

My mother, Pauline Nāwahineokala'i Evans, was one-quarter Hawaiian. As a young child, she would often accompany her mother on visits to Queen Lili'uokalani during the years following the overthrow of the Hawaiian kingdom. One day, when my mother was only about five years old, the queen offered her an apple, which was a special treat, and coming from the queen! My mother smiled sweetly and said, "I have four brothers."

My mother met my father when he was going to McKinley High School and she was going to St. Andrew's Priory, the Episcopal school for girls. They were married in 1912, and my mother joined him in the Philippines, where he was assigned to the U.S. Navy's Asiatic Fleet.

When I was born, there was a question about what my baptismal name would be. My mother and father argued all the way up to the steps of the church. She wanted me to be Samuel Wilder King, Jr., and to call me "Junior."

"Absolutely not," my father said. "He's got to have his own name."

They compromised. I became Samuel Pailthorpe King. Ormand Cleveland Pailthorp was my father's best man and Annapolis classmate, who died in a shooting accident a month before I was born. (I spell it with an e and he didn't, I found out later.) I don't have a baptized Hawaiian name. I don't know why. In fact, I'm the only member of our family of five who doesn't.

Dad was fairly strait laced. I remember one story my parents told about a time in Hankow when they were playing tennis. There was a naval officer who was trying to make time with the wife of another officer, who was out on the river. Dad didn't say hello. Eventually this guy came over to my dad and said, "Oh, Sam, I haven't met your bride." My dad stood up and put his hands behind his back and said, "I do not choose to recognize you." He was serious.

But he had a very soft heart. He never hit us. He left the discipline all to my mother. But apparently they got together and agreed on what it was going to be. He'd say, "What does your mother say?" But he knew what she was going to say because they had talked about it.

I inherited that sense of right and wrong from him. Later in life, I got a lot of my basic feelings about racial justice, opposition to the death penalty, and, of course, being a Republican and fighting for statehood, from him. Like him, I'm an open-minded optimist, and people have said we both have a liberal streak. Maybe I do.

When I attended Yale College, my mother was alarmed when I told her I was a pacifist, an agnostic and a Communist. She told my father, who had been napping. He shrugged, and before he turned over to go back to sleep, he said: "Don't worry. It's like measles. He'll get over it."

In many ways, I did. ❧

Chapter Three

SAMUEL WILDER KING

My father had a remarkable life: Successful businessman, delegate to Congress from Hawai'i, appointed governor of Hawai'i, ardent proponent of statehood, and a Navy officer with service from Japan and the South Seas to dangerous crossings of the Atlantic Ocean during World War I. While this is my memoir, it wouldn't exist without the inspiration of my father, Samuel Wilder King.

He was born in Honolulu on December 17, 1886. Mostly Scottish, he also had some Hawaiian blood from his mother. He could read and speak Hawaiian and would sometimes make campaign speeches in the language. He became the first governor of Hawai'i with Hawaiian ancestry.

My father had a tremendous influence on my life, politically and personally. One example is my opposition to the death penalty. Another is the way he handled himself. People trusted him, and they valued what he had to say. He typed an Abraham Lincoln quote onto his stationary and hung it on his office wall; now it's on mine:

> *If I were to try to read, much less answer, all of the attacks made on me, this shop might as well be closed for any other business. I do the very best I know how—the very best I can; and I mean to keep doing so until the end. If the end brings me out all right, what's said against me won't amount to anything. If the end brings me out wrong, ten-thousand angels swearing I was right would make no difference.*

I'm sure the main reason I became a Republican was because of my father's example. I think he believed that, at the time, the Republicans were the party of common sense, which is what probably appealed to him. And it didn't hurt that the man who got him into the Naval Academy, Prince Jonah Kalaniana'ole Kūhiō, was a Republican, too.

After graduating from McKinley, known at the time as Honolulu High School, my father went to work for the Wilder Steamship Company, working interisland routes. He knew every little stop around the Islands. He had amazing knowledge of the whole territory. His father, James A. King, had been port captain for the company and I'm sure that's how he got the job.

Ironically, my grandfather was not all that happy about seeing my father take a job that put him on the ocean regularly. Their oldest son, James, had been lost at sea—some kind of squall in the Pacific. All they found was a life preserver that had come from the ship. It just broke up my grandfather.

One day, dad ran into the high school principal, M. M. Scott, a very fine man who was responsible for encouraging a lot of youngsters to do more than just deteriorate after they got out of high school.

"Sam, what are you doing?" the principal asked my father.

"I'm working for the steamship company."

"Sam, you're wasting your talents. You should go to Annapolis."

That got Dad thinking, and pretty soon Principal Scott was talking to my dad's parents and one of his grandfathers: "This is terrible, you know. He ought to go on with his education. He's wasting his talents, and the thing for him to do is go into the Navy."

In those days, you didn't have to take entrance exams. My father got appointed to Annapolis in 1905 by the Territory's congressional delegate, Prince Kūhiō, who was a good Republican. My father was the second part-Hawaiian appointed to Annapolis; the first was from California. I like to say he liked it so much that he went for five years. Actually, he bilged—what they called flunking—the mechanical drawing class.

My father wasn't very religious, but Catholic churchgoers at Annapolis were allowed to leave the base to go to chapel each Sunday, because there wasn't a Catholic church on the grounds. He loved getting away from the base, so that was his religious period. He never missed a Sunday.

After graduation, he had an active Navy career that took him first to the Philippines with the Pacific Fleet and then China and later to the Atlantic, where he helped ferry supplies past German U-boats to Great Britain.

Dad left the Navy when World War I ended, and returned to Hawai'i, where he started a successful real estate business, focusing on the booming suburb of Kaimukī. "Have a Kingdom of Your Own" was his slogan—$500 a lot. He had a Japanese partner who would build houses on the lots once they were sold. But politics was in his blood, and he soon managed an appointment to the Honolulu Board of Supervisors, while maintaining real estate and insurance businesses.

In 1934, he won an election as Hawai'i's delegate to the U.S. Congress, beating a prominent Democrat named Lincoln McCandless, who was also in real estate as well as the tourism business. My father immediately began campaigning for statehood. Hawai'i's economy revolved around the plantations, and business leaders pretty much pulled the strings in Washington, D.C. Dad felt strongly about getting more power to the people, even though that did not always help him politically.

Dad had a strong civil libertarian streak. On at least three occasions, he was part of a delegation to Washington on behalf of Hawai'i. He argued in Congress against imposition of martial law following the notorious Massie murder case, he fought tirelessly for statehood and he opposed the mass relocation of Japanese residents following the attack on Pearl Harbor. In each case, his cause prevailed, although statehood took quite awhile to complete and required the efforts of many. And the relocation of AJAs [Americans of Japanese Ancestry] was not found unconstitutional until many years after he died.

It was the follow-up to the Massie case that kind of projected him into politics. The courts in Hawai'i had convicted an older Washington socialite, Grace Fortescue, and three other haoles of murdering a Hawaiian man—who, along with several other local boys, had been accused and later acquitted of raping the woman's daughter, Thalia Massie, a Navy wife stationed in Hawai'i. Even though Mrs. Fortescue never served any real punishment for the conviction, Navy brass and some key people in Washington were furious. They seemed to assume that the case was really about race, and that whites in Hawai'i could not expect equal justice. Take, for example, this quote from Navy Admiral Yates Stirling, after the first trial ended in a mistrial:

> *"I was informed reliably that the voting began … and remained to the end, seven for not guilty and five for guilty, the exact proportion of yellow and brown to whites on the jury. In Hawai'i, every jury will be Asiatic or mixed blood with a sprinkling of Hawaiians and whites. Ordinarily, civil justice can be obtained. In this extraordinary case, the emotion of the races has been aroused to a pitch where sympathies were in favor of the accused men."*

The drumbeat for imposition of martial law stepped up. The general assembly of Kentucky, Mrs. Massie's home state, passed a resolution urging President Hoover to obtain justice for her and, if that was not possible, to declare martial law until such time as "Hawai'i can be made safe for women."

A law was introduced in Congress to put Hawai'i under Navy control, just like Samoa. Terrible! The Navy was very strong for it, and I suspect some would still be today, although they would deny it!

The Territorial government sent an Equal Rights Commission to Washington to try and stop it: My dad, Justice A.J. Robertson and Senator

Bill Heen. They got the proposal deferred for a year, and, by the next year, the steam had kind of come out of the idea. You might say that was a step toward statehood. Although that push for martial law failed, it came back after the Japanese attack on Pearl Harbor and lasted, in my opinion, at least, far longer than necessary.

Partly in response to the Massie case, my father was a very strong champion for statehood and introduced a bill for statehood in 1935. In testimony before the House Committee on Statehood in 1935, my father said:

"Are we to be found lacking through fear or suspicion of our people without just cause?

"Is a community whose young, formative years have been thoroughly American to be judged in advance as to their loyalty when every item of evidence shows its complete assimilation of American ideals?

"In all sincerity, as one with 20 years service in the Navy and a wide acquaintance with Mainland communities, I doubt if there is under the American flag a more loyal part of America than Hawai'i."

Dad served three terms in Congress but withdrew right after Pearl Harbor to return to the Navy as a commander, and later became captain. My father's second round of Navy service took him to Saipan, American Samoa and eventually aboard a ship assigned to Japan to repatriate American prisoners of war. After the war, he returned to Hawai'i, where he busied himself with politics and the pursuit of statehood.

Dad felt strongly about the need for statehood. He was one-eighth Hawaiian and very proud of it. He resented that we were only a territory and had no political representation, whereas all the states had two senators and more power to control their own destinies. Congress could do anything it pleased to a territory—declare martial law, for instance—and it wouldn't have any say in the matter. He had a very low opinion of most of the congressmen, especially the ones from the South. Back in those days, you got off the airplane in Atlanta and everywhere you looked, it said whites only, blacks only. He didn't want people who came from that mentality making decisions for Hawai'i.

After the war, he returned to Hawai'i where he busied himself with politics and the pursuit of statehood. He served as chair of the so-called "Hope Chest" Constitutional Convention of 1950, at which we wrote a constitution to prove to Washington that we were ready for statehood. He was also a member and later chairman of the Statehood Commission, from 1947 to 1953.

At one point, my dad got a House of Representatives committee that had been considering statehood to make an inspection trip to the Islands. That hadn't happened in a long, long while. The committee members had a great time. Earl Thacker, who was in real estate and tourism, drove them around in his fancy car and they got to meet Duke Kahanamoku and ride a canoe off Waikīkī. I got the impression they said to themselves: "Gee, why didn't we do this before?" After that trip, they came every year!

In 1953, my father was appointed governor by President Eisenhower and served until 1957, when he lost his political backing. I know a lot of it was because of the unions. He had testified against the ILWU [International Longshoremen's and Warehousemen's Union] in some of the anti-Communist trials, and he helped organize the independents when there was a dock strike. He gave speeches against [ILWU regional director] Jack Hall. When Harry Bridges and the other union leaders wouldn't let a ship full of medical supplies be unloaded—saying that "a little suffering will do 'em good"—my father hired independent workers to unload the boat. It didn't break the strike, but it made the unions mad. So they were hot to cut his throat, politically at least. And at the same time, many of the interests who had supported him kind of drifted away—the plantations and so forth. They weren't looking for a fight with the unions.

One day, with little notice or explanation, the U.S. secretary of the interior called him and said he would not be reappointed governor. He asked who was going to succeed him, and they wouldn't tell him. So what was he supposed to do? Sit there like a lame duck? "You don't want me?" he said. "If so, I'll make it easy for you. I'll resign." And he did, the very next day. They didn't expect that. Young Bill Quinn, out of St. Louis, replaced him. I never had any personal problem with Quinn, but my dad thought it was an insult to Hawai'i to have some guy from St. Louis see us into statehood. Instead of just slinking away, Dad turned around and ran for the Territorial Legislature and got elected outright in the primary in his old Kāne'ohe district.

His interest in statehood never flagged. In March 1959, Dad was in the hospital suffering from emphysema and other ailments. He had smoked almost all his life. He was recovering from an operation and they were having a hard time getting him out of the anesthetic. The doctor came to him and said, "Sam, Sam, we got statehood!" He smiled. His dream was achieved.

Two weeks later, he died. ❧

Chapter Four

INNOCENTS ABROAD

Growing up, I always seemed to have the good fortune of being in the right place at the right time. By the time I graduated from law school in 1940, I had traveled across the Mainland and throughout Europe, which not many kids from Hawai'i were able to do. I'd met the president and the pope. I'd even seen the famous fan dancer Sally Rand. And all of this, I saw through one eye. That was because of my father, but it wasn't his fault. It was an accident. It also probably saved my life.

We moved from China when I was about six months old. The United States had just entered World War I. My father was assigned to running destroyers in the Atlantic, taking supplies to Europe. I remember briefly being in Philadelphia, then ending up on Yerba Buena Island in San Francisco Bay. It's now called Treasure Island. The bay wasn't polluted in those days, and the island had good dirt. My older sister, Charlotte, made the best little mud pies, which we ate. We came home to Hawai'i after World War I. My father had been assigned to duty at Pearl Harbor, the 14th Naval District.

I was six years old when I lost my eye. I was watching my dad with great interest as he opened wooden crates. He hammered a hatchet into the boards and pried them up. That's when a little piece of steel came off the hatchet and went in the middle of my left eye. I lost sight in that eye immediately. I'm sure the Lord did that. If I hadn't lost the eye, I would have gone to Annapolis like my Dad. It turned out that it was members of what would have been my class who died aboard the cruisers that sank near Guadalcanal during World War II.

I could see out of my good eye, and a person really only needs one eye. I like to tell a joke about a one-eyed banker. The glass eye, the banker would say, is the one with emotion. I did lose some depth perception, but it never really hampered me much. It made me money in grammar school: I'd take out my glass eye and charge the other kids two bits to see it.

We grew up in Kāne'ohe where my dad bought some property at Halekou, across the street from where Hawai'i Memorial Park is now. He subleased the property to relatives and friends. It was a close-knit neighborhood, with great views of Kāneʻohe Bay.

Although we lived on the Windward Side, the only elementary school was Central Grammar in Honolulu, known today as Central Middle School. We didn't have the Pali Tunnel in those days, so it was a long trip to and from school. The school days were even longer for a couple of years, because, after classes at Central, my sister Charlotte and I were sent to Japanese school at the Hongwanji Mission School on Judd Street. I didn't want to go, but my father thought you should learn a foreign language.

There weren't too many non-Japanese kids, and the teachers were pretty strict—like all teachers in those days. I'm left-handed, so naturally I would write the *kanji* [writing system] with that hand. The teacher would try to make me write with my right hand, but, because I wasn't Japanese, she didn't bother me too much. At that school I learned *katakana* [a form of syllabic writing], the way a sentence is formed and quite a bit of vocabulary. It would later help me during World War II.

When I graduated from Central, which went up to the seventh grade, I was supposed to go to Lincoln Intermediate. But Lincoln was an English Standard School, and my father didn't like the idea of two separate public school systems based on how well kids could speak English. He made a lot of noise about it: "That's absolutely terrible. You ought to treat all citizens alike. These kids are all American citizens." It hurt the Japanese kids, and Hawaiians, too.

My mother and father felt that the only thing to do was to get out of the public school system, so we applied to Punahou. That's why I learned French. To get in, you had to know a foreign language. Japanese didn't count. I finally passed the French exam and got into Punahou. Once there, I took four years of French, and another four years in college.

At Punahou, things came easily to me. I ended up in all sorts of activities. I didn't have a steady girlfriend, but I won just about every honor they had. At the end of my first year, they had an election for the president of the junior academy. One of the candidates was Elizabeth Cooke. After the election, she congratulated me for winning and said, "I voted for you." I asked her, "Didn't you vote for yourself?" "No," she said, "I wouldn't do that." Naturally, I had voted for myself.

I was on the track team. My best time in the mile was four minutes, fifty-nine seconds, which was good enough to go to the state meet and finish fourth. I also competed on the four-mile relay team, which still holds the high school record here, mostly because the event was discontinued. I also went out for the varsity football team, but the varsity coach wouldn't let me play.

He said, "You only have one eye, and you'll get injured." I played anyway, for the intramural Punahou Blues team, center on offense and tackle on defense. I was also in ROTC and was president of the rifle team. I was a crack shot. I told people it was because I didn't have to close my left eye. I later got elected student body president.

During the summer I got jobs as a rodman with the Territorial survey office. My first assignment was to check on the subdivision of Moloka'i homestead lots. As part of that assignment, I was sent to Kalaupapa—we called it the leper colony—to check on improvements to the houses. We had two Hawaiian boys with us, and one had a sister there. He was really anxious to see her. We stayed about a week and they tried to keep us separate from the residents. Even at the movies, they had a separate place for us to sit. But I knew you can't get leprosy from shaking the hand of a leper, so I didn't hesitate to shake hands.

Among my family's closest friends was the Reppun family—the one whose descendants still grow taro in Waikane Valley. They were very cultured people. They would speak Russian and French at the dinner table so their kids would hear that. I learned to play chess from them, and I've played it ever since then.

Once when I was on the federal bench, I played a match with a young reporter who also loved the game. We exchanged a move each day. During one court hearing, the lawyers were arguing matters that they had already cited in their briefs. So I wrote a note on a piece of paper and gave it to my law clerk, to give to the reporter in the gallery. As the lawyers were still talking, the clerk delivered it. The reporter looked at the note and then just sat there for a little while—I think he was being polite to the lawyers. Then he left. The note said something like B-B4, which meant moving the bishop to a particular square. I don't remember who eventually won that game, but, if he says I did, I won't deny it.

My brief career as a foreign correspondent was the result of my foray into high school acting. The acting teacher urged me to enter the Damon Speech Contest, which I won. When the National Oratorical Contest came up, I entered and won the Territorial finals held at McKinley High School auditorium. It was a big deal in those days. The *Honolulu Star-Bulletin* sponsored the contest and the top prize was a trip to Washington, D.C., to represent Hawai'i in the national finals, plus a tour of Italy, France and Switzerland. You could talk about whatever you wanted to, but the *Star-Bulletin* was paying for it and its publisher, Joe Farrington, was very much for statehood. I came up with "Hawai'i—An Integral Part of the United States." *Star-Bulletin* editor Riley Allen offered some suggestions and corrections to my talk, and I worked with the guy who was in charge of stage and drama stuff at Punahou. We developed the theme "Hawai'i: The Forty-Ninth State," or something like that.

The newspaper stories were headlined: "Punahou Youth Wins Honors in Oratory Tests" and "Samuel King is victor in final oratory event." Seido Ogawa from McKinley High School came in second, and Ruth Aki from Kaua'i High School placed third.

Allen wanted me to send articles from Europe that his newspaper would publish. They would be headlined, "To Europe with Sam King." A picture of me would accompany the articles. So there I would be, a seventeen-year-old kid from Kāne'ohe, writing about my travels to Europe. An accredited newspaperman!

I left Honolulu on May 6, 1933, still a Punahou senior. "I am started today on a trip to Europe, made possible by the *Honolulu Star-Bulletin*, with the right to represent Hawai'i in the finals of the National Oratorical Contest at Washington, D.C.," I wrote in the first published dispatch. "I sailed on the *Malolo* at noon with a very gratifying sendoff and wish to take this opportunity to thank all those who bade me bon voyage either physically or spiritually. The tears welled up in my eyes as the wharf began to slip away and I did not try to stop them."

I chronicled each day of the trip beginning with how I was happy I didn't get seasick, and my visit to San Francisco. In Chicago I got to see what was considered very risqué for those times: Sally Rand, the exotic fan dancer. There was an exhibit at the Century of Progress World's Fair just for her. I was too young to go inside, so I watched her from outside a fence. The women were wearing brief shorts, but otherwise, they were naked. They threw balls back and forth. Then there was Sally Rand. To me, the fan dance was a real joke. She had these great big fans, and she waved them around and never showed anything. Of course, I didn't put that in my dispatches, just as I didn't report everything we did in Paris.

In Washington, D.C., I got my first taste of watching Congress in action as it debated a Hawai'i statehood bill, which didn't pass. "All in all it was most interesting," I wrote. "The Senate is much better ordered than the House, where personal insults are hourly occurrences."

The national speech finals were held at Constitution Hall, which was similar to McKinley's auditorium. I wasn't nervous. I knew the people in Hawai'i supported me. "I come to you tonight from a land five-thousand miles away," I told the audience. "It is a group of islands in the mid-Pacific, swept by fresh trade winds, green and lovely under the tropic sun, sparkling in a sea of azure and emerald." Remember, this was in the days before television, the

Top: Baby Sam and amah, *Hankow, China, 1916.*

Bottom: Aboard the steamship Malolo *in May 1933, Sam departs for San Francisco on his way to Washington, D.C. and Europe.*

Top: Sam and his mother, Pauline Evans King, in 1970.

Bottom: The King family ca. 1946. Front row: Samuel Wilder King, Pauline (Hine) King, Pauline Evans King. Middle row: Evans Palikū King, Charlotte King McAndrews, Anne King. Back row: Davis Mauliola King, James McAndrews, Sam.

Ensign Samuel P. King in 1944 at the U.S. Navy Japanese Language School in Boulder, Colorado.

As Territorial government leader Hebden Porteus looks on, convention chairman Samuel Wilder King (right) signs Hawai'i's new constitution at the Constitutional Convention of 1950.

Four years later, at Honolulu's John Rodgers Airport, Governor King, congressional delegate Joseph Farrington and Honolulu Advertiser *editor Buck Buchwach (left to right) help load a massive pro-statehood petition bound for Washington, D.C.*

Top: Governor King joins U.S. Vice President Richard Nixon in greeting Japan's Crown Prince Akihito.

Bottom: Governor King and U.S. Senator Hiram L. Fong, here in 1958, were longtime leaders of Hawai'i's Republican Party.

Top: Sam and Anne King's three children in 1953 (left to right): Charlotte (Becky), Louise and Sam, Jr. Sam kept this photo on his desk.

Bottom: Sam at 'Iolani Palace in 1968, accompanied by (left to right) his younger daughter, Charlotte (Becky), wife, Anne, and mother, Pauline.

The King family on a Chinese junk during an around-the-world vacation in 1964.

Anne and Sam on the occasion of Sam's taking Senior Status as a federal judge in 1986.

Anne and Sam celebrate their 65th wedding anniversary in San Francisco in 2009.

In 1994, the King family gathers at Kaimana Beach. First row: Sam W. King II, Nāwahineokalaʻi
Lanzilotti, Anne Lanzilotti, Charlotte Stretch, Sara Stretch, Becky King Stretch, Adrienne King.
Second row: Anne, Sam, Louise King Lanzilotti, Salvatore Lanzilotti, David Stretch,
Sam King, Jr., Chris King.

Internet or the Pearl Harbor attack. Hawai'i was a far-off, exotic and mysterious place that many Mainlanders didn't even know existed. "Once peopled only by brown Polynesians whose blood flows in my own veins, it is now a territory of the United States. It is a strategic point in the great Pacific area, a harmonious melting pot of many races, and is a part of our common country. It relies upon the principles of the Constitution for a full measure of justice. It is on that Constitution and its immediate, its vital bearing on Hawai'i today, that I speak to you."

I did my best but didn't place. John Phillips of Kansas City won the title Champion Orator of the United States. The Honolulu newspapers ran an Associated Press story saying I made "an exceptionally fine showing," and added that I drew "a brisk round of applause" for a talk that was "clean-cut and forceful."

I also added a Hawai'i touch: I placed a yellow-and-blue paper lei around each winner's neck. That also generated a lot of applause. "I went to bed content," I wrote in my article about the contest.

While I didn't win, I did get the consolation prize of a trip to Europe—all the finalists did. Off we went: Phillips, George Oliver from Florida, Perry Dornans of Oklahoma and a young woman with the unlikely name of Rosemarie Cauliflower. Plus our chaperones, of course.

I continued my writing from Europe. Editor Allen liked what I sent him, but, just like all editors—at least that's what reporters I know tell me—he had a complaint: "These letters are mighty interesting and many people speak about them," he wrote to me. "But, *please* write on one side of the paper only. It is difficult for the typesetter to follow your story when it is written on both sides of the paper."

On August 1, 1933, I met Pope Pius XI at the Papal Palace, the most magnificent place we had seen on our European trip. Our audience was set for the afternoon. The ceremony was simple. "We sat on benches in a long hallway that was crowded with people of all nationalities, walks of life and probably religious beliefs," I wrote in my dispatch.

After about an hour of waiting, the door opened at the far end from us. A troop of Swiss guards dressed in bright yellow and red uniforms and Robin Hood hats marched down the hall. They were followed by another group of aides, a clergyman of high rank and, finally, the pope.

"He was dressed in white robes, white skull cap and wore glasses," I wrote. "He is a small man, apparently gentle and scholarly. He passed down one side of the hall and back the other side, holding out his right hand on which was a ring that each person kissed in succession."

There was an embarrassing moment for me when he got to us. Here's how I reported it: "I'm afraid we boys made an awkward spectacle, when we rose after kneeling too soon, I caught the bench with my legs and caused a terrific clatter. Also, when the priest preceding the pope asked John (a fellow national oratorical finalist) if he was from New York, and when the pope uttered one word, 'Americans?' Perry (another finalist) verified the statement by going down the line naming our home states, much in the manner of a Pullman conductor." When the pope reached the end of the hall, he gave us his blessing and left. Next stop: Paris!

Paris had a well-known—what's the word?—"reputation" for naked women and all that sort of thing. So, along with one of the other guys on the trip, I wanted to see all this stuff. There we were: two innocents abroad. We saw the advertising for this show, so we went in to see it. Looking back on it, it was pretty routine. They didn't give out very much and we were too young and scared to get into close contact. But every show they had that we could get into, we went and saw.

I didn't return to Hawai'i from Europe; I went straight to Yale. I never attended my own Punahou graduation, but they left an empty seat for me on the stage. By then, I guess I had become enough of a celebrity that the newspapers reported I had won a scholarship. My father and mother were very appreciative of that, and I know Dad also liked that I went straight from Europe to New Haven, which meant he didn't have to pay for another trip between Hawai'i and the East Coast.

When I got to Yale, I stayed in the top room of a walk-up with two other students. I understand that Nathan Hale—the man who said, "I regret that I have but one life to give for my country,"—had lived in the same room in the 18th century. One of the other students was a guy from New Haven, Doug Yerxa, who became a very dear friend. He later went to war as a pilot and kept saying he wanted to get to where the action was. He was shot down and killed two weeks before the end of the war in the Pacific. The other roommate was Richard Sutton, who later ran for office in Hawai'i as a Republican.

I joined the Yale debating team, and it was through the team that I met President Franklin Roosevelt and his wife Eleanor. Two debaters and I went to Georgetown University in Washington, D.C. The debate topic was Roosevelt's New Deal. One of the debaters was the son of a woman who had political connections in the Democratic Party and somehow got us into the White House. Mrs. Roosevelt had said: "There are three of them? Tell them all to come."

We were to be the only guests at lunch with Mrs. Roosevelt that day, the anniversary of the president's first year in office. Then the president rolled in, in a wheelchair. He asked us what we were doing in Washington, and we told him we were there to debate the New Deal and had been assigned the case against it.

"Oh, how did you make out?" he asked.

"We lost," I said.

"Eleanor, they lost!" he said. The president threw his head back and laughed uproariously.

Although we argued against the New Deal, I personally was for it; I thought of myself as something of a Communist. I blame it on my Yale education. In those days, most of academia was left-leaning pacifists and atheists.

There was no way I couldn't have been a Republican because of my father, but that didn't mean I had to disapprove of everything President Roosevelt was doing.

The president had to go back to work after lunch, but Eleanor was very nice and more than gracious. She went out of her way to show us around, and she even took us to the president's office.

I ended up with a Bachelor of Science degree from Yale. I went in that direction because I had top scores in math and physics at Punahou. They sorted out students based on what they thought was your aptitude. I took even more aptitude tests at Yale. They all showed I ought to be either a preacher or a lawyer. I didn't have too much interest in becoming a preacher, so I applied to Yale Law School and got in. I really enjoyed it. I found the study of law fascinating, and I didn't do too badly. I worked on the school's law review and became a member of the Order of the Coif, reserved for the top 10 percent of graduates.

I graduated from Yale Law School in June 1940. By that time, my views were already changing. Religion is a funny thing. My father began life as a Catholic, but not really a devout one. My mother was an Episcopalian, who went to St. Andrew's Priory; her mother was one of the original members at St. Andrew's Episcopal Cathedral. When my father married my mother, he became an Episcopalian, and that's how I was raised.

My views about religion changed when I went away to school, and then changed again when I grew older, especially when we had our three children. In the Sermon on the Mount, there's a reference to that: Throw the devils out of the house but make sure something is there, because if you don't, new devils come in. Sure, the kids may not believe in what Episcopalians believe, but they've got to have something in their minds that you're comfortable with. And whether they reject it is up to them when they get old enough.

At any rate, the views on Communism, pacifism and atheism I had acquired in the ivory tower were about to be tested. We were going to war. ❧

Chapter Five

THE WAR YEARS

When the Japanese attacked Pearl Harbor on the morning of December 7, 1941, I was asleep in Honolulu. I was a relatively new lawyer and was living at the Mānoa home of my Uncle Bill, Dad's younger brother. My cousin Billy came in my room and said, "Sunny, Sunny. They're doing maneuvers. Let's go take a look." My childhood nickname was "Sunny Bunny," because of my optimistic nature, I suppose.

I jumped out of bed and got dressed. That's when a neighbor yelled, "Turn on your radio! Turn on your radio! The Japanese are attacking!"

On the radio we heard Webley Edwards say the famous line, "The Rising Sun has been sighted on the wingtips." The authorities came on and said, "Stay home. Don't go parading around, making things worse."

We could see airplanes from our house, but the attack didn't last all that long—maybe an hour and a half. My immediate reaction was that the Japanese military had blundered into a losing conflict with the United States. I said to Uncle Bill, "The timing is all wrong." If they had not attacked us, we would probably still be arguing about whether to declare war on Japan and Germany. Admiral Isoroku Yamamoto agreed with me in recognizing that the attack had awakened a sleeping giant.

Even after that attack, the Congress was not quite unanimous in its declaration of war. Congresswoman Jeannette Rankin of Montana refused to believe that the Japanese had bombed Pearl Harbor. She thought it was all a public relations trick by President Roosevelt. My father, who was Hawai'i's delegate to Congress, spoke to her at the request of the House Speaker, to tell her that he had already talked to me by phone and that the Rising Sun had indeed been seen on the wings of the attack planes.

"Is it true?" my father asked me during that phone call.

"Yes," I replied.

"Well, anybody we know of been hurt?"

"Nobody that we know."

Then he asked about Bobby Jarrett's folks in Kaimukī, but that's when the line went dead. They cut us off. The censors were already on the job.

Congresswoman Rankin still voted no. War against Japan passed the United States House of Representatives 434 to 1.

Everyone, it seemed, had known the attack was coming except the Navy and the Army. The skipper of a commercial ship named the *Steel Trade*r returned from the Orient shortly before the attack, and reported that all the talk in Japan was about going to war with the U.S. He even tied up in Honolulu with short lines so he could take off and go to sea as soon as there was an attack. This guy was absolutely furious that the military was unprepared for an attack.

Their arrogance did them in. They thought, *Japan can't come to Pearl Harbor. It's too far away.*

I had returned from Yale in 1940, taken the bar examination and taught high school mathematics at Punahou for a semester while I waited on the bar results. Shortly after they came out, I was sworn in as a lawyer. My first job was with the Territory of Hawai'i, the Rights of Way Department. I was in charge of writing attorney general opinions. It was mostly administrative stuff, but I enjoyed it, and it was good work.

One opinion that stuck out was whether or not the contracts between Hawaiian Home Lands lessees on Moloka'i and the pineapple companies were authorized by federal law. I concluded that they were not. The attorney general agreed with me, but nobody paid any attention to us. The companies went right ahead and did what they were going to do anyway, covering land that was meant for Hawaiians to live on with acres of commercial crops.

I later started working as a deputy prosecutor in the police court of the City and County of Honolulu, handling traffic tickets, assault and battery, petty thefts.

That all changed the day after the attack. The military declared martial law—illegally, by the way, in my opinion—and took over everything, including the territorial and county courts. They brought in military prosecutors who didn't know what they were doing, and changed all the laws by executive fiat. I told my boss to take me off the payroll because I wasn't doing anything.

What I wanted to do was enlist, but because I had only one good eye, I needed special permission. Somebody told me it could only be gotten in Washington. So, in April 1942, my dad and I caught a military aircraft and headed east. Just outside of Los Angeles we came under antiaircraft fire. I could hear the pilot yelling "Hey! Wait a minute!" He finally got through to the ground and convinced them we weren't enemy aircraft. Luckily, they missed. I guess my guardian angel was watching out for me.

When people ask me if I was ever under fire during the war, I say, "Yes." But then I tell them the rest of the story.

My dad, however, was under hostile fire at least once. He landed at Saipan during the battle. He commanded what was called an "ACORN" (Aviation, Construction, Ordnance, Repair, Navy). They would go in right after the Marines and take care of all the crap that had been landed on the beach.

In Washington, I managed to get a waiver for "absence, acquired, left eye," and found employment in the Legal Division of the War Shipping Administration. Before long I applied for a Navy commission in intelligence, and was commissioned an Ensign, I-V(P), U.S. Naval Reserve, on September 1, 1942.

My first assignment was to report to the Eighth Naval District in New Orleans, Louisiana. What a joke. The Navy assigned me there because I could speak French. Only one problem with that: They don't speak French in New Orleans. They say they do, but they speak Creole. There was another problem: My job was to examine people coming into the United States. Most of them came from South America and spoke only Spanish or Portuguese.

The French Quarter had been shut down, but life otherwise remained warm and friendly. We read about the war as we attended the New Year's Sugar Bowl game. You couldn't tell that a war was going on.

I was looking for ways to work my way back to the Pacific when, in early April 1943, a circular arrived announcing the "Enrollment of Special Navy Language Students" for instruction in the Japanese language at the University of Colorado. Enrollment questions were referred to Lieutenant Commander A.E. Hindmarsh, USNR, in room 4631, Navy Department, Washington, D.C. I had no clue as to how I got on the mailing list. I had also never heard of Boulder, Colorado, where the school was located.

But because I had gone to Japanese school as a kid in Hawai'i, I wrote Professor Hindmarsh and began brushing up on *katakana* and *hiragana* [the two Japanese syllabic writing forms] and general vocabulary. I took leave and went to Washington, D.C.

My interview was conducted by Glenn Shaw, who had composed winning *haiku* when he was the U.S.'s cultural attaché in Tokyo. His grandson would become a member of the Hawai'i State House of Representatives.

Shaw handed me *Naganuma Book One* and told me to read and translate the first sentence. I don't know if he did it on purpose, but he gave me the book the wrong way. So I turned it over and opened it properly, from the back. I skipped over the pages of *kana*, and noted that the first sentence was in *katakana*, which I could sound out, except for one *kanji*, which I didn't know.

The *katakana* read *"kore wa* [unknown character] *desu."* I knew that the word for book was *hon*, so I confidently recited, *"Kore wa hon desu*: This is a book." That was the end of the interview. I was in.

About two weeks later, I was ordered to report to the Navy's Japanese Language School at Boulder. Because I was the only student in an officer's uniform, a rumor soon circulated that I had been sent to the school to report on any un-American propensities of the other students. I was promoted from ensign to lieutenant junior grade, mostly because of the passage of time. It tended to fortify my position in many minds as a spy for Navy intelligence, but my classmates eventually got over that.

We worked hard and learned what we were supposed to learn. The first groups to complete the program included most of the BIJ [Born in Japan] students who already spoke Japanese. A few of the last BIJs were at Boulder in my group, but most of the students were starting from scratch. None of these were of Japanese ancestry while I was there. Many of the students had grown up in Japan because their parents had business interests there or were American missionaries. The Army had recruited most of the Japanese Americans, and I was with the Navy. One exception was Douglas Wada of Hawai'i. He was the first person of Japanese ancestry to receive a commission in the U.S. Navy, and he interpreted at the highest Navy levels. The *sensei* [teachers], however, were all of Japanese ancestry; some were even Japanese citizens.

Then the Navy decided to bring to the school about 100 WAVES. That's Women Accepted for Volunteer Emergency Service. I was given the pleasant task of commanding them in close-order drills in Japanese.

Among them was a lovely young woman named Anne van Patten Grilk. Annie was born in Hinsdale, Illinois, but, when her father died, her mother took the family to Exeter, New Hampshire, where she was raised. She majored in Greek and was a Phi Beta Kappa at Smith College. That's how she got into the Japanese-language program. The Navy wanted Phi Beta Kappas, and she read about the program in the organization's journal. Annie looked good, coming and going, and she was exactly what I wanted: "brains and beauty."

My roommate, a guy named Danny Karasik, had taken Annie out a couple of times, but then he graduated and left Boulder. Not long after that, some of us made a trip to Washington, D.C., and were on our way back to Boulder. We were in the club car on a train coming out of Chicago on the way to Boulder, and I saw that one of the WAVES had a dirty white cap cover. Her name was Tyson.

"Tyse, you've got a dirty cap cover," I told her.

"Well, I don't have a clean one," she replied.

Annie was with her. She said she had a clean one and got it for Tyson.

"Good deed," I told Annie. "I owe you a beer."

She took offense at that remark, but I was with a bunch of guys and didn't pay much attention.

I was attracted to Annie but didn't have the courage to follow up. But then, some time later, I was at a Boulder drugstore, eating my breakfast, when Annie came in to get something to eat. She commented on my breakfast of chocolate donuts and coffee, and then, as she left, she said, "You owe me a beer."

A few days later I called her, and we starting going out. I proposed two weeks later.

Her one-word response was the Japanese word "*Maa*," which means "yikes," or "heaven forbid." She said that she didn't believe in wartime marriages.

"But that's the only kind there is in wartime!" I pleaded.

That was a Sunday. She told me to ask her again on Wednesday.

I don't worry much, but when I'm asked about the last time I lost sleep worrying about anything, I say it was between that Sunday and Wednesday.

When I proposed again on Wednesday, she accepted.

On July 8, 1944—about two weeks later—we got married in Boulder, in a big ceremony attended by our classmates and instructors, some of whom were Japanese nationals. It's a good bet not many American weddings around that time included Japanese nationals as honored guests! Annie's mother also managed to get there, traveling by train, which was quite an accomplishment during wartime.

One of the big sports in Boulder was water polo, and the university hosted other Navy programs for men headed for duty in the Navy or Marine Corps. An energetic lieutenant whose duty was to keep everyone physically fit decided to start a water polo program with teams from each unit. He invited the Japanese-language students to participate. We accepted the challenge, with me as the captain. I asked him what the rules would be.

"Oh," he almost sneered, "there will be no rules." He added that we could withdraw if we did not want to play without rules. Evidently, the Boulder language students were assumed to be pantywaist intellectuals.

But, as luck would have it, our program included some champion speed swimmers, former water polo players, and men who had grown up in and around the sea. Of course, we murdered the other teams, almost literally. With no rules, we could take an opponent under water and hold him there while our speed swimmers rushed down the pool and scored. Our participation in sports with the other training units ended abruptly.

Another diversion was the Japanese board game Go. Some of our *sensei* were highly educated Japanese nationals who happened to be in the U.S. when Pearl Harbor was bombed. One had been an officer in the Japanese navy. He loved to play Go and would hold game sessions during free hours. I stumbled upon one of these sessions and was immediately hooked. I never could beat him, but I was fascinated by the game.

Back in Hawai'i after the war, I played every Saturday with the strongest player of Go I could find: *Sensei* Inagaki. He was a waiter at O'ahu Country Club who helped me hone my own skills. Eventually I was invited to meet visiting Go champions from Japan, and I once played a game by telephone against a champion player in Japan. She was in a Tokyo department store and I played from the meeting room of a Honolulu hotel. I won.

In the course of studying Go, I heard about the first treatise on the game in the non-Asian language. It was by O. Korschelt and appeared in a serial form in German publications from 1880 to 1884. I obtained a microfilm copy of the series from the Library of Congress and collaborated with Annie's mother, who read German, and with retired Professor George G. Leckie, who had translated German mathematical works. I also checked questions about the game itself with my Go *sensei*. All this took years. Charles E. Tuttle Company published the finished product in 1965 as *The Theory and Practice of Go*, by O. Korschelt, translated and edited by Samuel P. King and George G. Leckie. A paperback came out in 1990. I still receive modest royalties.

I sometimes wished I *had* been a Navy spy at the language school. Then I would have had access to the biographies of the other remarkable men and women who passed through the school and the equally remarkable *sensei*. One of the teachers was Professor Okamoto, whose daughter, Barbara Marumoto, later became a member of the Hawai'i State House of Representatives.

The Boulder experience indeed had a profound influence on my life. I would gladly go through it all over again.

I was discharged from there on July 1, 1944, and ordered to report to the Advanced Naval Intelligence School at 353 West 57th Street, in New York City. Annie was assigned to the same section, but the boss cautioned us not to socialize too much during coffee breaks, as this would be bad for the morale of the unmarried officers.

The work was routine. Nothing we were asked to translate had immediate operational importance. My most important decision was to dispose of a copy of an Army report on dissatisfaction among Navy personnel in the Aleutians. I figured it had nothing to do with translation, so why keep it? A month later, a very nervous Army major arrived to retrieve the report. "Oh, hell," I said. "I put it in the burn basket." He seemed relieved, and he had me sign an affidavit saying our copy no longer existed.

Before long, I was ordered to report to the Joint Intelligence Center, Pacific Ocean Areas, Hawai'i. I was going home! By this time, Annie was no longer in the Navy. She got kicked out because she was pregnant. They don't do that anymore, and Anne didn't want to leave, but those were the rules.

We came to Hawai'i on the Matson ship SS *Matsonia*. I reported for duty on June 30, 1945, as a translator. The war was still going on, but the curfew, which had been in force since the Pearl Harbor attack, was lifted shortly after our arrival. For most of the forty-three months that the curfew had been imposed upon the people of Hawai'i, it was unnecessary. In fact, it was wrong. The military had kept the curfew as a method of control of the local population, not out of military necessity.

The lifting of the curfew was a signal that the war was moving closer to Japan. There were rumors that Japan would be invaded, in which case many of us Boulder-trained Navy types would be assigned to Marine forces in the initial landings. Deadly. Then came the atomic bombs over Hiroshima on August 6 and Nagasaki on August 9. I remember reporting to work and being told to take the day off because there were developments about the war. We packed up our pencils and went home.

As I was walking in the door of our rented house, the telephone started ringing. What followed may read like a conversation, but it was actually a series of orders.

"Hello?"

Voice on the other end of the line: "Is this King?"

"Yes."

"Are you going to Okinawa?"

"Yes, sir!"

"Are you leaving first thing tomorrow?"

"Yes, sir!" ❧

Chapter Six

IN THE LAND OF THE RISING SUN

The Japanese were about to surrender. I was on my way to Japan where I saw firsthand the atomic devastation that brought the war to an end.

I was ordered to join the USS *Adams*, a minesweeper that had departed without a Japanese language officer on board. I was transferred to the USS *Harry F. Bauer* for a high-speed chase of the *Adams*. We met the *Adams*, to which I was transferred by breeches buoy on September 2, 1945."

As we approached the Japanese mainland, formal surrender ceremonies were being orchestrated further north in Tokyo Bay. The commanding officer called me to the bridge and told me to get on the bullhorn and instruct a waiting Japanese minesweeper to go south, away from the event. That was the first Japanese I used in communicating directly with the enemy. After they obeyed my first set of orders, I instructed them to send over a boarding party. Then I readied myself for the important task of interpreting whatever they would have to say.

We quickly saw that these poor guys had run out of everything, including fuel. But they had with them a wizened old harbor pilot who spoke something like fourteen languages, including beautiful English. They needed me like they needed a hole in the head.

What happened next is typical of the Navy, or of the military in general. Our captain noticed I wasn't that busy, so he called me in and said, "You know I don't like people not to be doing anything, so I want you to meet ships that want to come into the harbor and tell them how to get here."

"But I don't know anything about navigation," I said.

"Just tell them to stay in the middle of the channel and they'll be all right."

So there I was: King the Navigator. My father and grandfather were legitimate navigators, but I wasn't. I just played the part: "Stay in the middle of the channel and you'll be all right." Luckily, no ships were lost.

Some of the Japanese soldiers were fire-eating *banzai!* guys who hated Americans. I remember encountering one early in my stay in Japan. The Marines had landed at Tokyo, but, where we were, the cargo ships came in first. I was ordered to go ashore and tell the Japanese forces, "Stay out of our way." I got into a speedboat and went shore-side. I found a booth with a telephone someone had set up and I called up the Japanese forces and told them in Japanese, "We're the Americans and we don't want any interference." They said they'd send the man in charge down to meet me.

This guy shows up at the wharf and it was clear he was trying to intimidate me. He put his finger on my collar insignia and said, in English: "Oh, Lieutenant." I was obviously not of high enough rank to deal with him. So I put my finger on his insignia and said, in Japanese: "Oh, Commander." He was furious.

The Japanese authorities quickly replaced the hardcore types with ones that were quite sophisticated. These smooth guys did the waltz, spoke better English than I did Japanese and knew exactly what we needed.

While I was there, I was assigned to accompany a group of high-ranking officers and scientists to get a firsthand look at Hiroshima. People have often asked me if I was worried about going to where we had just dropped the bomb, and I always say, "No, I was too dumb to worry."

On our way to Hiroshima, we stopped at a port south of Tokyo and who should be there in charge of a ship assigned to remove American prisoners of war? My father! He didn't know I was there, and I didn't know he was there. I got to have lunch with him. He was so delighted.

While I was on Dad's ship, I saw some Americans who had been prisoners of war in Japan. They looked terrible. The crew made them take all their clothes off, dumped all kinds of disinfectant on them and gave them something to eat—but not too much or it would all come up again. As my father pointed out, nothing could be worse than to stuff them with food. Even so, I thought to myself: *Jeez, they're treating these guys worse than the Japanese treated them!*

Hiroshima was total devastation. We didn't see any dead bodies, because they were just gone. Obliterated. The place was deserted. There wasn't much for me to translate since everything had been blown away. We walked around—these top officers and me—and I remember seeing one sign still standing and an officer asked what it said. "It says 'tobacco,' Sir," I answered.

I couldn't help thinking as we walked around that—as horrible as it was—if it hadn't been for Hiroshima and Nagasaki, I likely would not have survived the war. I probably would have been assigned to the Marines who were to land at Hiroshima and you know how the Marines are: "Gung ho! Let's go! Let's get 'em out!" It would have been bloody.

After the mine detail, I was assigned to a team that included a red-bearded physics professor from Bryn Mawr, someone from the U.S. Geographic Survey and me. The three of us were supposed to go to all the ports and survey what was there.

We got as far as Tokyo and couldn't go any farther without permission from General MacArthur. That held us up in Tokyo. Tough duty. Everyone was very friendly—the Japanese people, as opposed to the tougher wartime officers. They were 100 percent cooperative. They treated us less as liberators and more, actually, as tourists. If there were some who wanted to spit on us, they made sure they weren't around. My main conversation, everywhere we went, was with the guy who was representing the government. Each one would offer us a bunch of women.

The women were not necessarily willing. The government official would just say: "You, you and you over there. Let the Americans have you."

"No! No!" we'd say. "We are prohibited!"

We stuck to our mission. One of our assignments had to do with the Japanese attempt to split the atom and perhaps create atomic weapons. They had two cyclotrons but not the latest. Nonetheless, on orders from Washington, General MacArthur insisted that they be broken up and dumped into Tokyo Bay. The guy in charge of our group—the physics professor—got very upset. He was absolutely at wit's end. "No," he said, "we can't do that."

I don't know if he was concerned about the loss of science or the possible harm to the environment, but in the end, they did get dumped, and to this day Japan doesn't have nuclear weapons.

During that period, I received two telegrams. The first one I got said our child had died. The second telegram notified me that a baby daughter had been born. I guess the two got crossed up in transmission. The poor thing. She was born with an abnormality and the doctors were unable to do anything about it. When the command learned about this, they offered to let me go home to take care of Annie as soon as I wanted.

"Now!" I said.

Soon after, I was discharged from active duty, although I remained in the reserves for many years. It was time, now, to launch my civilian career. ❧

Chapter Seven

AVAILABLE JONES

I owe a lot to the cartoonist Al Capp. Two of his Dogpatch characters provided me with my most memorable nicknames: Available Jones and Marryin' Sam.

Available Jones was the L'il Abner character who would do anything for a dollar. "Minding Babies: dry, 5 cents; other kinds, 10 cents." That's the name I gave myself when I first started law practice, right after I returned from my six months in Japan.

I wasn't down to minding babies, but at the start of my legal career I was up for almost any other business that came my way. I set myself up in the back of my father's real estate office. Annie became my secretary, and I was in business. My first month, I think I made $185. We found a piece of property on Old Pali Road, and Annie applied for a G.I. loan so we could buy it. We built a very small house, which soon had to be enlarged. Annie was pregnant again, and within a few months her opu wouldn't fit under the typewriter in our office. A secretarial agency sent me Rebecca Yamashita (who later became Rebecca Berry), who worked with me for most of the rest of my career. A son was born, Samuel Pailthorpe King, Jr., and then two daughters in quick succession: Louise Keali'iloma and Charlotte Lelepoki.

When you're starting out and your family is growing, you have to take on whatever comes your way. I even defended Annie in a traffic case once! I found that far more tickets had been given to women than to men, and so I argued that the law treated men and women differently. We won that one.

I had one case where my client was accused of being part of a burglary gang. He claimed he was asleep in the back of the car at the time of the incident. I took it to the jury and they let him off. As he was walking out of court, he was rearrested for another burglary. The cops said, "We've got about fourteen more here." I only represented him on the first one.

A lot of the work was routine, but there were a few cases that stick in my mind even to this day. They include the glamorous Filipina women and the Japanese patriots.

The Filipina case involved two sisters from a well-to-do Philippine family who were stopped at customs and accused of smuggling jewelry from the Philippines. I think they were on their way to Europe after a stay in Hawai'i. Customs had them dead to rights, since they had all this jewelry in their luggage and had not declared it. But I argued that they weren't smugglers—they were simply carrying their own possessions. Well, the court bought it and they were let off. Before long, they were off to Europe. Unfortunately, they didn't have the money to pay me but they promised they were good for the bill.

Not long after, I was visited in my office by their brother, a fine-looking man with an excellent record as an officer in World War II, who had come to Hawai'i to settle up their problems. He said, "I know we owe you money and I would like to pay you with this." And then he brought out some very nice jewelry that for all I know he might have smuggled in from the Philippines. I think I accepted a ring for myself and one for Anne.

The Japanese patriots were another wild case. At the beginning of World War II, there was a lot of suspicion about the loyalties of Japanese living in Hawai'i and on the Mainland. As far as I know, there wasn't a single case of espionage or treason ever confirmed by the United States government. Not one. But on the Mainland, as everyone knows, tens of thousands of AJAs—Americans of Japanese Ancestry—were rounded up and relocated to camps in the interior of the Mainland. Hawai'i was more fortunate. Relatively few AJAs were relocated, and many served loyally in the military or in civilian jobs during the war years. But it would be wrong to assume some Japanese didn't retain some loyalty, or love or affection for their home country. I would, for sure.

So I got this case on appeal: At the end of World War II, there were stories in the local newspapers of the Allied victory and photos of American troops marching down the Ginza in Tokyo. These three old bucks, Japanese immigrants who did not speak any English—Shizuichi Yamamoto, Seiichi Masuda and Kichibei Sueda— were living in Hilo. They saw a photo and mistakenly thought it was a parade of captured U.S. soldiers, and that Japan had won the war! They thought, "American forces would never be marching like that through Tokyo unless they were under control of the Japanese military." So they got excited, went outside and raised the Rising Sun flag. I guess they were members of the "Never Say Die" society.

So of course they got arrested for raising an enemy flag in a time of war. General MacArthur was in Japan, and the Japanese had already surrendered, but the formal peace treaty had yet to be signed. Anyway, we had a statute that made what they did a crime. The government even subpoenaed the son of one of them to testify that his father had raised the flag.

The lawyers who represented them couldn't handle the case on appeal. So I took on the case, along with Ed Silva, who later became attorney general. We went over to the Big Island and made all kinds of arguments and appeals: "The regulations don't work, they weren't passed in a timely manner," and so forth. It shouldn't be illegal to raise the Japanese flag, for God's sake, but we were technically still at war at the time.

Martin Pence, with whom I later served on the federal bench, was the appeals judge. After hearing our arguments, he came back in fifteen minutes and declared he was denying the appeal. But, at the same time, he commuted the sentence to a small amount of money and time served. So none of them went to jail. Pence and I used to laugh about that case later. He had his decision written even before we showed up in court. This was justice tempered with mercy. The odd thing is, I never met the Hilo "patriots." They were old and they didn't even speak English.

During the twenty years I was a private attorney, I also got involved in some issues that might have left my Republican friends—and my father as well—wondering where my true loyalties lay. One such issue involved two of Hawai'i's best known and loved political liberals, University of Hawai'i Professor Alan Saunders and his wife, Marion Hollenbach.

This was in the late 1940s, and, as the rest of the nation, Hawai'i was embroiled in a fury of anti-Communist sentiment. This was the McCarthy era, and politicians everywhere, from Congress to the local school board, were on the lookout for Communists and Communist "sympathizers."

Like my wife, Marion was a former Navy WAVE. At the time of the so-called Hollenbach case, she had married Dr. Saunders, already a respected University government professor. Marion, an educator, kept her maiden name, although she later became well known as a Board of Education member and education reformer under her married name, Marion Saunders.

Her husband, Professor Saunders, was an ardent critic of the anti-Communist movement, specifically criticizing the U.S. House Committee on Un-American Activities. He was also the Hawai'i representative of the American Civil Liberties Union, as well as a member of the liberal Americans for Democratic Action, all of which made him a target for the anti-Communist groups then active in Honolulu. Marion, who was then involved in the statewide Parent Teacher Association, became a target as well in a classic case of guilt by association.

I knew Marion because we had collaborated on training workshops for the PTA, where I was brought in as an expert on parliamentary procedure. I later got to know and like her husband when, in 1966, we both served on a legislative committee on penal law reform. As I wrote in a chapter for a book on Dr. Saunders produced by University of Hawai'i Press: "He, a staunch Democrat, and I, a staunch Republican, were usually in agreement."

I considered Marion a friend and was outraged when officials tried to oust her because of who her husband was and her own supposed pro-Communist leanings. And believe it or not, she was also attacked for choosing to use her maiden name professionally! Marion was anything but a Communist; like myself, she came from a staunch Republican family and was a loyal Navy reservist. When I learned about what was happening to her I called up and asked whether she had a lawyer. She said she didn't. "Well, you do now," I said. And I sat down with her and prepared a letter rejecting the absurd charges that had been set against her.

I had a lot of fun as a private attorney, but it became clear my destiny was to be a judge.

The qualities that make a great judge do not necessarily make a great lawyer. A judge doesn't have to know anything, as long as he's honest, educated and willing to listen, because he gets the best lawyers to tell him the law. Whereas a really top-notch lawyer would probably make a lousy judge. It requires too much contemplation. He wants action.

My first full-time job as a judge came in 1961. At the time I was working as executive secretary—kind of a legal advisor—to the State Senate president, Doc Hill, a Republican from the Big Island. It was a Saturday and I was walking away from the Capitol—'Iolani Palace in those days—and I ran into Bill Quinn, the Republican governor, who was also headed home. "Sam, Sam," he said, "you want to be judge of the First Circuit Court?" His question caught me totally by surprise, but I kept my cool and said, "I have to check with my wife."

"Well, I have to know soon, because it's an immediate decision," Quinn said.

When I sat down with Annie and my good friend Bill Stephenson, they both urged me to take it. So I told Quinn I would do it, and on Monday he sent my name down to the Senate. Soon I get a call from George Ariyoshi, then in the Senate and, of course, later our Democratic governor. "Don't worry about a thing, Sam," he said. "I'm voting for you, and that gives you 13 votes." And I said: "Oh, thank you very much," but I didn't know that he had just fixed a problem. There were Fourteen Republicans in the Senate at that time, and twelve said I was a good appointment. But two, Randy Crossley and Yasutaka Fukushima, who I had known at Yale Law School, said they were holding back until they could take a few things up with the governor. When Ariyoshi said he would vote for me, that gave me the thirteen votes I needed.

I know exactly what happened. Bill Stephenson got ahold of Bert

Kobayashi, who was a fellow district magistrate and a good friend of mine and of the Democrats. Kobayashi got to Ariyoshi and told him, "You gotta come out for King." And he did. In fact, Kobayashi came to my rescue many times over the years. He later served as Governor John A. Burns' attorney general.

I gave myself the Available Jones nickname. The other Al Capp moniker, Marryin' Sam, was given to me. As a Family Court judge during the 1960s, I presided over literally thousands of marriages. Pan American Airlines published a book for tourists that read: "If you want to get married, call Judge King, known as "Marryin' Sam." According to my figures, I officiated at over 2,199 marriages. I'm sure a few of those involved famous folks, but I never asked questions about that sort of thing.

In my years as a state court judge, I also handled more than a few divorces, probably as many divorces as marriages. Sad record in some ways. If a couple stipulated they were married and now wanted a divorce, and if both sides agreed—uncontested—then I granted it.

I don't remember granting the divorce of the parents of President Barack Obama, but that was apparently the case with them, because I signed the papers they filed.

Sometimes, people change their minds. I remember one case. This gal wanted to divorce a young man and it was uncontested, so I was ready to sign. But then, when the soon-to-be ex-husband died suddenly, her lawyer called up and said, "Don't sign it! Don't sign it!" I tore it up and she got the man's money as his widow.

Of all the things I did during my years on the state bench, I'm proudest of my efforts in partnership with Judge Gerald Corbett, a Democrat, to create the Family Court system in Hawai'i, which became a model for other states. Before we got involved, domestic issues from child juvenile delinquency to divorce and domestic abuse were handled in the criminal or civil courts, scattered here and there. Our idea was that these issues could be better handled in a sensitive manner outside of the regular system of justice. There were objections, of course, but we knew how to handle them: When a Democratic legislator would complain that this was "King's idea, coming from the Republicans," Corbett would say, "No, it's my idea." And when any Republican would complain that this was the idea of that Democrat Corbett, I would say, "No, it's my idea." We got it through, and Hawai'i's Family Court system became a national model that's still followed today.

One of the things I was most concerned about was the previous pattern of putting juvenile offenders into criminal court. In most cases, I thought that was just plain wrong. I remember writing a letter to the papers once in 1969 after State Senator Duke Kawasaki attacked the Family Court, and Corbett in particular, for being too lenient on juvenile offenders. I was particularly offended because Kawasaki used a speech I had given—arguing for more support for the Family Court—to buttress his argument. I said, and still believe, that treating youths as adult offenders and incarcerating them, rather than providing concerned involvement by social workers and others, is a big mistake.

Once the new Family Court that Judge Corbett and I campaigned for was off and running, I was invited to lecture on family court matters at the National College of State Trial Judges (now known as the National Judicial College) in Reno, Nevada, where new state judges from all over the country were sent to learn the ropes. I continued to serve on the faculty there for many years. You don't educate judges; you just suggest things. It was a summer program, and I enjoyed talking to all these eager newcomers to the bench. In some states they were elected, and in others they were appointed. The elected ones thought the appointment system was better and vice versa. Only the ones from Missouri were satisfied with their state's plan.

No system of selecting judges is perfect. For example, the process by which I got to the state bench might seem rather informal and political, and I guess it was. But it was no worse than the system we have now. In many ways, it was better, because back then the politics was out in the open. Now it is hidden behind the Judicial Selection Commission. But don't kid yourself that there isn't politics going on all the time in the selection of judges. There is nothing wrong with open politics. People will always operate politically. It is human. The problem with Hawai'i's current judicial selection system is that it operates in total secrecy. The Commission should be abolished. As far as I am concerned, the entire state court system is tainted by politics.

Even when I was there, on the state court, there was lots of funny business. For example, it used to be a big deal to be the one in charge of the probate calendar. You got to appoint your friend as an appraiser, and he or she might get as much as $5,000, which was a lot of money in the 1960s, without needing to have any expertise at all. It was a sweetheart deal. Just about every member of the Senate got one of these appointments from time to time.

Pure politics. I didn't want any part of it. ❧

Chapter Eight

TERRITORIAL POLITICS

I was in and around politics for most of my life, or at least until the day I became a federal judge. My early political career included doing errands for my dad. You could say I was his right-hand man. When he was appointed governor of Hawai'i and I was working as a young lawyer, I'd slip in through a side door to his office at 'Iolani Palace and see him just about every day.

I'd deliver messages and do whatever he needed to be done. For example, he said: "Go see Judge Steiner and find out if he wants to be a circuit court judge." "Yes, sir!" I asked Judge Steiner and he said, "No, I'm happy where I am, head of district court." I took that message back to my father.

Another time, before he was governor and was serving as chairman of the Republican Party, there was a Constitutional Convention called the "Hope Chest" convention because it was supposed to demonstrate that Hawai'i was ready for statehood. My father wanted to serve as chairman of the convention. So I'd go around and spread the word that my father should be chairman. And that's what happened.

My political career became much more intense after I became chairman of the Hawai'i Republican Party in 1953, replacing Randy Crossley. I don't know whether that bothered him or not, but I know he was upset the next time we crossed paths. That was when Dad was appointed Territorial governor instead of Crossley, who had apparently been promised the job.

Delegate Joe Farrington was called in by President Eisenhower's secretary of the interior—the agency that was responsible for the Territory of Hawai'i—and was told "We're going to appoint Randy Crossley." My dad thought Crossley was not a good choice for the job. When he heard about it, he said, "Well, that's terrible." Crossley was a relative newcomer to Hawai'i and he was backed by powerful, hard-nosed California interests who had a lot of influence in Washington. It was the same group that backed Richard Nixon in his career.

Because Joe Farrington's mother had just died, Farrington asked if the appointment could be put off until he had a chance to return to Honolulu for the funeral. By coincidence, Crossley was his seatmate on the flight back to Hawaiʻi. As soon as he arrived, there was a meeting at my house in Nuʻuanu with Farrington, Hiram Fong, my father, me, Hebden Porteus and a few others. Farrington opened the conversation by saying: "I don't think he's got it." Hiram asked: "What are we going to do?" My father said, "We fight." Hiram added: "We can't be any worse off if we fight than if we don't, so let's fight."

At the same time, Crossley let it be known that he wanted to see me. I went down to his place at Diamond Head. He wanted to offer me the number-two spot as lieutenant governor, but I declined. "Randy," I said, "I'm sorry you asked to see me because now I can never accept anything from you. It would always be said that I sold out my father. "Besides," I said, "you haven't been appointed governor yet and it's my prediction you're not going to be."

That ended the meeting on a sweet note.

We got busy working on behalf of my dad. One of Dad's Japanese supporters came down and donated a thousand dollars to send telegrams on his behalf. I called every Republican precinct chairman around the territory and asked each to send a telegram. Meanwhile, a committee of six United States senators who had served in Congress with Dad called on the president to express their support for him. The interior secretary instructed his son-in-law, who lived in Hawaiʻi, to do a telephone survey to find out what people felt about Crossley and King. One of the people he called was a close Japanese friend of my sister, who called me and said: "Hey, this man wants us to give names to him so he can call them up and ask who they want to be governor." We gave her lists of names with lots of Dad's friends on it!

Crossley later went on to run unsuccessfully for governor in 1966 and in 1974.

While I like to think I did a good job helping my dad get appointed, and that he was the best person for the job, national politics was doubtless involved in the choice as well. My father was a strong Robert Taft supporter and backed him at the 1952 National Republican Convention even after it was clear Eisenhower had the nomination sewed up. Ike's decision to appoint my father was reportedly a gesture toward Taft. In any event, it was only after Taft died that Dad was replaced as governor by Bill Quinn.

This was in the early 1950s, and then the Democrats famously had their "revolution" and took over the Legislature. Just about everyone says this was a turning point in Hawaiʻi politics. Since I was chair of the Republican Party at that time, I guess you could say I was the guy who lost the state for the Republicans.

But, from my perspective, it was all but inevitable. The Republican Party wasn't attracting new people, because, if you wanted to get anywhere, the wisest thing to do under the circumstances was to be a Democrat, because most appointed governors up until Ike were Democrats. Republicans had a hard time getting appointed to anything important in politics. Beyond that, they kept putting up the same old guys for office, while the Democrats had energetic young local kids, just back from the war and college. There was some new blood in the Republican Party, including Hiram Fong, who later became a U.S. senator. But they had trouble getting past the incumbents. We did get a few of the AJAs, but most of them went to the Democrats on the simple theory that opportunities for quick political advancement were better there.

In the years since, it has been said that the young AJA vets and others went with the Democrats because they weren't welcome in the Republican Party. That's not entirely true. My dad appointed some Japanese to important positions. His press spokesman, Larry Nakatsuka, was the first AJA to work for the local paper and was probably the first person of Japanese descent to be a spokesman for a governor. The young bucks didn't have the power to take over the Republican Party, but they could take over the Democratic Party. They could build it from scratch without having to buck an "establishment."

In some ways, the Republicans were just worn out. Many of the best of our leaders were dying: my father; Joe Farrington, who was a delegate to Congress; Roy Vitousek, who had been head of the Republican Party. The Democrats have called that 1954 election a "revolution," but it wasn't a sudden sweep. If you look at the numbers, it had been creeping up gradually.

One of the reasons my dad was so interested in statehood was he thought that it might change the political tide. We'd had a long stretch of appointed Democratic governors prior to my father and Bill Quinn, and the Democrats were getting a lot of the patronage appointments from the Mainland. He thought we could do a much better job of selecting our own public officials.

When I talk about Republicans, I am talking about the ones I grew up with and worked with. They are not like the right-wing Republican conservatives we have today.

And what is a Republican and what is a Democrat in Hawai'i these days? Think of Burns and after him George Ariyoshi and then John Waihee—businesspeople loved them. They're as pro-business as they could be. Big business and big labor have gotten together under the Democrats. There's no longer that separation.

When I was growing up, Republicans were the party of good Yankee sense, fiscal and otherwise, and the absolute caricature of a conservative reactionary was a Southern Democratic senator, still in mourning for the Confederacy. The *Honolulu Star-Bulletin* writer Jim Becker recalled in a 1979 column that at a hearing at the old Territorial Senate chamber in ʻIolani Palace, a Southern senator visiting Hawaiʻi asked, "Governor, how do you handle your minority problems out here?" Becker wrote that my father responded, "Senator, in Hawaiʻi we are all in the minority." ❧

Chapter Nine

A Last Political Hurrah

My biggest political adventure was challenging Jack Burns for governor in 1970. There is no question that Burns and the Democrats had accomplished a lot in the preceding eight years, but many in the community—Democrats and Republicans alike—felt they had worn out their welcome. The growth they had encouraged was getting out of hand. With statehood came an influx of money and people, and skyrocketing traffic and organized crime, among other things. Many felt, as I did, the energy that had brought them into office had worn down. As I would say in my campaign, they were tired—too tired to deal with the multiplying problems of a new state.

In any event, I understood that Governor Burns was ill, and word was that he was unlikely to run for a third term. His lieutenant governor, Tom Gill, was expected to run for governor, and he wasn't nearly as popular as Burns. Gill was very smart, but he had a sour personality and a habit of making people mad at him. I thought I was going to run against Gill and felt I could beat him. But the Burns people were determined to shut Gill down at any cost. They decided to run Burns for a third term, in spite of his failing health.

I'm a strong believer in the "three-party" system: Republicans, Democrats and Incumbents. And the Incumbents almost always win. A bunch of people—Ed Brennan, Phil Spalding and others—asked me to run. As I always do, I asked Annie what she thought. She was opposed to it. We talked about it for a while. I told her a large part of my reason was that I was frustrated with my job as a state circuit judge under the late Chief Justice William S. Richardson. There's a reason that the judicial and legislative branches of government are separate, but the court under Richardson, who was a Democrat, clearly had a political, not a legal, agenda.

When Bill Richardson and I were relatively young men, during the decade or two following World War II, he made no secret of his political agenda. He used to say the game plan of the Democrats was to take over politics and then the court system, and finally Bishop Estate. I suppose that's why I always thought of Richardson as a politician, even when he served as chief justice and later as a Bishop Estate trustee.

I have to say, however, that some of his rulings, particularly on Hawaiian rights issues, were intriguing and most likely correct in the context of Hawai'i and its history.

One was the Richardson Court's ruling on beach access, which essentially said that the beaches belong to the public. Another was his ruling on gathering rights, that people who traditionally had gone up to the mountains to collect things could continue to do so, as long as it was on undeveloped land—that was a good ruling. I thought he was absolutely correct on that case where he ruled that lava lands, new lands created when lava flows into the sea, belong to the state.

I did have a little trouble with his ruling on water rights, that surface water cannot be owned by anyone. You can use it, but it basically belongs to all of us in common. That decision fit with his interest in applying a Hawaiian perspective to things, but it is far more complicated than how his court saw it. Over time there are competing interests as to who wants the water and what they might use it for. It keeps changing. It's not that simple.

I would never say that Richardson didn't make some interesting decisions. But, at the same time, he was a dedicated Democrat and he politicized the entire court. People used to say, "Don't take a case to the Supreme Court if you can help it. You'll get a political ruling."

By the 1970s, Richardson was beginning to treat the Family Court that Gerry Corbett and I had helped found like a political football. When Gerry died, someone needed to be appointed head of the Family Court. I was the logical choice, because I was the only one there. But Richardson took a brand-new judge and named him chief of the court. That was all right with me, but, when the judge left the bench, Richardson found someone else to name as the chief.

When Annie heard this, she changed her mind and said, "Well, if you want to run for governor, go ahead." It was the only time I proceeded with a big decision without Annie's wholehearted approval.

I might have thought I was imagining things, but after I declared my candidacy and stopped being a state judge—you can't do both at the same time, of course—Richardson personally fired my secretary, Rebecca. Nobody had ever done that to a judge who left office. The chief justice had always reassigned the secretaries to work for someone else or had them wait until another judge was appointed.

I had already declared my candidacy when Burns announced he would run for a third term, mostly to keep Gill out of the governor's office. I knew it would be an uphill battle running against not only an incumbent but one who had the sympathy of the voters because he was in poor health. That didn't stop me from trying.

In my campaign for governor, I first had to get through a Republican Party primary against state Senator Hebden Porteus. Heb had staked out a very conservative position that I felt was not a good fit for the local Republican Party at the time. Even before the primary was over, I was already focused on the record of the incumbents: "Burns and Gill have yawned in the face of a record-high cost of living, an alarming crime rate, clogged highways, an acute shortage of housing and a sudden statewide drug problem," I said.

Sound familiar? You could give much the same speech today. But it wasn't just an attack on Burns-Gill. I talked about setting up a special task force on crime, wiping out the four-percent excise tax on food and medicine, creating a no-fault auto insurance system, building a new sewage plant at Sand Island, building a mass transit system to get cars off the road, using federal and state financial leverage to build affordable housing for seniors and low-income families, and improving education through increased construction of new facilities.

This was 1970, so, for some people, the influx of drugs and hippies from the West Coast was a major concern. I insisted that marijuana should not be legalized, as popular as the idea was at the time. I was convinced from my experience as a Family Court judge that marijuana could lead to the use of heavier drugs. I did say that first-time possession of small amounts of marijuana should be treated leniently.

One of the most colorful and, for me, painful moments of the campaign came late in the contest when the Porteus campaign effectively accused me of being soft on marijuana users, adulterers, criminals and hippies! The attack came in a campaign brochure entitled "Compare," which purported to compare my positions with his on these high-profile social issues.

Heb quoted me as saying, "I do not think possession of marijuana should be a crime," but I hadn't said that. I'd said that the sale of marijuana should remain a felony, but that a first arrest for possession of small amounts of marijuana should be a misdemeanor. It didn't make much sense to incarcerate a bunch of kids for trying pot. Our country's last three presidents have admitted to trying it.

Heb said I wanted to welcome the West-Coast hippies who had started sleeping at our parks and beaches as "refugees." What I'd actually said was that the police, who were reluctant to evict them because they had no place to go, should set up a place for them to report and find work.

Heb also implied that I was soft on criminals. He quoted me as saying

I would "never send anyone to jail if I could help it." What I actually said was that I would never send anyone to *prison* if I could help it; there is a big difference that perhaps Heb failed to understand. Jail is for misdemeanor defendants awaiting trial. The kinds of people you find in jail are completely different from the kinds of people you encounter in prison, which is for criminals sentenced for felonies. Our prison system is rotten. It needs to be reformed so that we don't throw purse-snatchers in with rapists and axe murderers. It's easy to say you want to "get tough on crime," but that recurring slogan fails to describe the underlying problems or provide for the return of offenders to society.

The misquoting didn't stop there. I had said that I thought common-law marriages—in which a couple who has been living together for many years can enjoy the civic privileges accorded to married people—should be legal. I'm not sure how Heb got from there to adultery, but he used the quote to spread the word that I thought it was OK to cheat on your spouse! Not the same thing at all.

All this seemed like a frantic last-minute effort designed by his advisors and advertising specialists. It didn't work.

Meanwhile, I kept up my fire on the Democrats. I recall a press release concerning a controversy over a member of the State Land Use Commission who made a fortune by rezoning his own property and later selling it for a fantastic profit. It was all over the papers. I called for a strong state ethics law and then commented, "In one respect, I find myself agreeing with both Governor Burns and Lieutenant Governor Gill. Burns says Gill can't be trusted. Gill says Burns is surrounded by corruption. I am sure they are both right!"

Another time, Gill challenged Burns and his people with contributing to a "slow and insidious loss of momentum in Hawai'i." I said I couldn't agree more, but pointed out that Gill, as "first mate," had no right to blame everything on the "captain."

I also took on Burns for one of his more memorable sayings, one that people remember to this day. Burns was pressed on why he wouldn't commit on some issue or another and he said, "My job isn't to take stands. Any damn fool can do that." Well, I disagreed with that then, and I do today. It is not only a public official's responsibility to stand up and speak out on the issues, it is his duty. In the primary election, I beat Porteus 20,600 to 17,900. Burns, of course, beat Gill. By then, I knew I had little chance of beating Burns and the Democrats in the general election, but I was determined to keep at it until the very last day.

Late in that campaign, a popular Democratic senator named Larry Kuriyama was murdered in the driveway of his 'Aiea home. Kuriyama had made organized crime a major issue, and his murder had all the earmarks of a gangland slaying. I gave a news conference in which I stated that if Burns had taken a stronger stand on organized crime, Larry Kuriyama "could very well be alive today and our state at peace instead of at war with organized crime." The Democratic Party immediately accused me of blaming Burns personally for Kuriyama's death, which of course I wasn't. But that incident certainly didn't help me in the election.

All the unions, except for the Teamsters, supported Burns. I know unions are naturally suspicious of Republicans, but they needn't have been in my case. I have always believed that unions serve an important role.

Another problem was my reluctance to promise things. One experienced politician told me that I should promise people whatever they wanted to hear. I couldn't do that.

Election Day came, and I received more votes than any Hawai'i Republican in a race for governor to that date, but it wasn't enough. Burns won by a count of 137,800 to 101,200.

In truth, I was disappointed, but I also felt a sense of relief. Losing the race for governor turned out to be the best thing that could have happened. During the campaign, I made a point of saying that I could work with a Legislature controlled by the other party, but the reality was that as a Republican governor with a Democratic legislature, I wouldn't have been able to accomplish much. As I said many times later, "I got lucky. I lost."

With politics out of the way, I went back to being a judge, but this time in federal court, and the most fascinating part of my life began. ❧

Chapter Ten

Sam King, Federal Judge

nnie and I were having a late weekend snack in our breakfast nook when the phone rang in early 1972. The caller was Senator Hiram Fong. He asked if I could come to his business office downtown on Merchant Street, which was only about a 20-minute drive from our Nu'uanu residence. I said I could leave immediately and did.

I was Hawai'i's Republican National Committeeman, and Hiram was Hawai'i's senior United States senator. President Nixon was on his way to China and would be arriving in Hawai'i for a one-day stop. So I thought that the Senator wanted to coordinate whatever would be done by the Hawai'i Republican Party to honor the president.

Hiram greeted me with a question: "Sam, do you want to be a federal district judge?"

He was asking me if I wanted to be one of two federal trial judges for the district of Hawai'i, succeeding C. Nils Tavares. He said he had a meeting scheduled with the president at the Marine Corps air base at Mokapu and he wanted to put it on the agenda. Then he added, "You'd be surprised at who else wants the job." He didn't expand on that statement and I didn't ask him to do so. We exchanged a few more pleasantries, after which I left and hurried home to report to Annie—there weren't any cell phones in those days. I was certain that she would be overjoyed. She knew I loved being a judge and disliked the politics of the state courts. The selection of a federal judge is a slow process. Several months later, I was teaching at the Judicial College in Reno when we got word that the Senate Judiciary Committee was ready to consider my nomination. I was to appear immediately. Annie and I flew to Washington, arriving in a downpour that had caused the Potomac to overflow its banks. Anyone in an unsafe area was advised not come into Washington the next day. Luckily for me, all the members of the committee appeared on schedule for the confirmation hearing, which came near the end of a long day of hearings. Senator Fong introduced me to the committee. Its members asked only a couple of questions and then confirmed me as a federal district judge.

It was faster and smoother than is normal, and I attribute much of that to Senator Fong. He was the first United States senator of Asian ancestry, and a man whose word was absolutely good. It also helped that Senator James Eastland, a long-time senator from Mississippi, had known my father when he was Hawai'i's delegate to Congress. I went up to speak to him after my confirmation. Annie whispered to me, "I bet he'll say, 'I knew your daddy.'" He shook my hand and said in his very Southern drawl, "Congratulations, Sam. I knew your fahthah."

I have always argued that judges, no matter how unbiased, cannot help but be influenced by their own experiences.

I'm part-Hawaiian, raised in these Islands, with what I guess you could call an Island mentality. My friends and my family, my education and my experiences, are all unique to me. How could that not affect my thinking?

This topic came up during the debate over the nomination of Sonia Sotomayor to be a Supreme Court justice. Sotomayor had given speeches suggesting that her experience as a "Latina woman" would necessarily color her conclusions in legal opinions. She later stated that she was "ultimately and completely" a judge who follows the law. I guess she had to say that, politically, but I'm not sure it was necessary. Almost everything worth arguing about is subject to interpretations, and that's where your experiences come into play. That's just the way it is.

Sometimes, the lack of experience can lead you to some pretty funny conclusions. I remember a case before the Hawai'i Supreme Court involving a bunch of Filipinos who had been arrested for cockfighting. Bernard Levinson, then an associate justice, reversed the conviction, saying the police had not shown that all these people were somehow involved in getting the cocks to fight. I ran into him later, and told him, "Bernie, those people were not there just to fight cocks. They were there to gamble. It's a gambling game!"

"Oh? It is?"

All the same, as a justice, you can't let your affections overrule the law. For example, I consider myself a true-blue Navy man. I was literally born in the Navy, served as a Naval officer during the war and spent most of my working life in the Navy reserve. Yet over the course of my federal career, I have ruled against the Navy and other military interests on more than a few occasions. I allowed complaints by war protestors who said they had been unfairly treated by military authorities, and I sided with defendants who were resisting military service as conscientious objectors. But the case that probably put me most at odds with the Navy—at least in a philosophical sense—was the Kaho'olawe trespassing case. It also produced one of the most unusual scenes I ever witnessed during my years on the federal bench.

It took place in May 1977, in the old Federal Courthouse. Two members of the Protect Kaho'olawe 'Ohana were accused of trespassing in an effort to stop the military from bombing that island. I like to keep things brisk in my court, but that day was likely the shortest session in history. I walked in to find a courtroom packed with people. They were all singing the state anthem, "Hawai'i Pono'i." Some were wearing the traditional Hawaiian *malo* [loincloth], and others were in ti leaves and gourd helmets—something they must have gotten out of books. I walked straight to the bench and declared, "This court is in recess." I then met in my chambers with the attorneys and the alleged trespassers. One of the trespassers, Walter Ritte, insisted that their garb was perfectly appropriate: "If we're not properly dressed, we should take down the statue." He was referring to the statue of King Kamehameha in front of the State Supreme Court building next door. It depicts Kamehameha in cape, *malo* and headgear. Interesting argument.

Then Peter Apo appealed to the Hawaiian in me: "For the sake of the Hawaiian people, please do not degrade us by telling us we are not properly dressed." I understood their point, but I still felt there had been an organized effort to disrupt the proceedings. So, Hawaiian-style, we settled our differences. They agreed not to disrupt the court and I agreed to let them wear their *malo*. With that, Apo asked me to join them in prayer. We formed a circle, joined hands and conducted our *pule* [prayer]. Apo said the words, and I added, "Amen."

You don't see a scene like that at the federal courthouse every day.

When we went back into session that afternoon, the case proceeded without further incident, although Samuel P. Kealoha, another of the defendants, insisted on calling me "Mr. America" rather than "Your Honor." He was representing himself, so I cut him some slack. He did fine, standing there in his Hawaiian garb, quizzing Navy officers who were all dressed in stiff white uniforms. In the end, I found Kealoha guilty of trespassing on the grounds that he knew he needed the Navy's permission to go on the island.

That was a key point: knowledge that the Navy formally demanded advance permission to go on the island. In an earlier, similar trespassing trial, with Walter Ritte, I had ruled for acquittal because I concluded that Ritte had not clearly understood that he needed Navy permission to land at Kaho'olawe. Walter had been among the original group to occupy the island. When the Navy picked him up after that earlier visit, he was tired, thirsty and somewhat disoriented. I wasn't sure he clearly understood at the time that he had been formally given what is known as a bar order, prohibiting him from going on to what was then military property.

I sympathized with their objections and acknowledged in court that many in Hawai'i viewed them as "popular heroes who crusade for justice." But

I added: "Society cannot exist if its laws are not enforced."

I should add I was always skeptical of the Navy's position that Kahoʻolawe was "the sole area which provides the training realism critical for our operational readiness." In 1990, after President George H.W. Bush gave that island back to the state, there was no effort by the Navy or anyone else to find another site. I guess the need was not so critical after all.

I also decided quite a few interesting cases related to the Vietnam War. Many involved conscientious objectors. Achieving CO status during the Vietnam era was no easy road.

One case involved an Air Force doctor named Lewis Chamoy, who had decided that he wanted out of the military. Air Force interviewers concluded that he was sincere in his application for CO status, but decision makers in Washington, D.C., said in effect that Dr. Chamoy was insufficiently sincere. They didn't like that his conscientious objections crystallized only when he wanted out of the Air Force.

Here's how I explained my decision: "It is sometimes a difficult task to distinguish between a conscientious objector and an unscrupulous opportunist; but when all those personally confronting the applicant support his claim and the only contrary arguments are speculations as to his state of mind, the court must find that no basis in fact exists for the denial of the petitioner's conscientious objector claim."

I don't see how people can easily accept the sincerity of someone who wants to get into the service and go to war, but then almost automatically doubt those who want out. Sincerity isn't just the province of patriots who want to serve.

One of my daughters and some of her close friends were conscientious objectors. They, like many others, went to Washington, D.C., to protest the Vietnam War. People have asked me if having members of my family strongly opposed to that war affected my thinking. It may have helped me keep an open mind. In any kind of controversy I try to assume that people are sincere, at least initially. In the end, I have to go by the evidence.

The draft dodgers who fled to Canada or elsewhere to avoid prosecution paid a high price. They were cut off from their former lives. I and a federal judge in New York ruled that federal charges against draft dodgers could not be maintained indefinitely, so we struck them all. Both of us were reversed on appeal, but the government did eventually grant amnesty to anyone who left the country over Vietnam.

I also presided over the trials of war protesters. One involved a group whose members were mostly from the University of Hawaiʻi, who wanted to protest both the Vietnam War and particularly President Nixon.

The president was flying into town to meet with Japanese Premier Kakuei Tanaka. Local Republicans planned a brass band and hula girls to greet him when he landed at Hickam Air Force Base. They invited the public to take part, and a bunch of the protestors went there to engage in "peaceful and law-abiding protest," as they later described it to me in the courtroom. They never saw Nixon, however, because Air Force personnel stopped them at the gate. Before long, the protestors had been fingerprinted, photographed and barred from coming through the gate. They sued the government, claiming that their constitutional rights had been violated and demanding money damages.

The government's lawyers wanted me to throw out the case. I wouldn't do that. I dismissed some of the claims, but I let the rest of the lawsuit proceed. I thought the protesters had a right at least to fight with the military in court, not just where the military might say they could fight.

The plaintiffs in that case—Willis Butler, Greg King, Ben Kerkvilet, Noel Kent, Melinda Kerkvilet, Oliver Lee and David W. Johnson—had made no effort to hide their plan to protest the president and the war, nor did they hide their identities when they were stopped at the gate. With them all that time had been a man known to the court only as "John Doe," who at the trial said he was an undercover agent. Kind of silly to infiltrate this particular group, since it made no secret of what it was up to. And federal officials claimed not to know who he was. Not too surprising, at least not in those days. ❧

Chapter Eleven

Cases Large and Small

I've had thousands of litigants come before me during my years on the federal bench. The smallest by far was a tiny yellow-and-gray feathered creature not much bigger than the palm of your hand. It was the palila bird, one of Hawai'i's many threatened or nearly extinct species. The biggest "defendant," in a sense, was the massive H-3, a billion-dollar federal interstate highway that pushes its way through the Ko'olau Mountains between Honolulu and O'ahu's Windward Side. The law and the weight of evidence caused me to rule in favor of both the palila and the highway, keeping their cases alive when the odds might have seemed stacked against them.

The palila case was the only one I know of in which the primary plaintiff is a bird. It is my longest-lasting case—I still receive annual reports on how the bird is doing. While it may have turned out to be something of a losing cause, I sided with the bird.

The palila is a finch-billed member of the Hawaiian honeycreeper family that has been listed as an endangered species since 1967. Its interests in the courtroom were represented by the Sierra Club, Audubon Society and Alan Ziegler. They wanted the bird to be the name plaintiff, and I allowed it.

When I wrote the first of many rulings in the case, the population of palila birds was somewhere between 1,400 and 1,600. The only place they lived was in the forests of mamane and naio trees between 6,400 and 9,500 feet on the slopes of Mauna Kea on the Big Island. Those forests are essential to the birds because the mamane trees provide food, shelter and nest sites. The naio trees are of secondary importance, but they also provide nest sites.

The State Department of Land and Natural Resources was maintaining a game-management area for hunters in the palila's critical habitat, and that created a problem. The population of about 600 feral sheep and 200 to 300 goats loved to eat the leaves, stems, seedlings and sprouts of the mamane trees and, to a lesser extent, the naio trees. This prevented the trees from growing and caused further decline in the palila population.

The palila's friends wanted me to protect the trees from those sheep and goats. The first thing they had to get past was whether it was in my power as a federal judge to tell the state government what to do, because there is a general prohibition against suing the state in federal courts under the Eleventh Amendment to the U.S. Constitution.

I ruled that, by actively participating in the conservation scheme and permitting the hunting of goats and sheep, the state had "impliedly consented" to be sued. I ordered the state to come up with a plan to save the palila by protecting the trees—or at least try to.

The hunters were pretty upset. They didn't want to eradicate the goats and sheep, which is what my order essentially required. The state dragged its feet, for the simple reason that hunters have more political power than birds do. So one day I mentioned in court, "Maybe I should take over the Department of Land and Natural Resources." I didn't threaten it. I just said "maybe."

The next day, the state had riflemen shooting goats from an airplane. Of course, the hunters got all upset again. The state still periodically shoots goats from helicopters, and it tries to maintain fences to keep the sheep and goats out.

I'm comfortable with my decision, though it didn't sit well with my friend and fellow U.S. District Judge Martin Pence. "Penny" had lived on the Big Island and loved to hunt. "You shouldn't have done that!" he told me. That didn't bother me. After all, he was a hunter.

It came down to enforcing laws passed by Congress to protect endangered species. That's a decision made by our elected representatives. Whether I personally agreed with the law was not an issue.

I still get reports each year on the number of palila. The last number was a couple of thousand or so, but it goes up and down. The question is whether there are enough of them to keep surviving. So far there are. I am pessimistic about the palila's chances for survival. But I was brought up to expect the worst, then be happy when it doesn't happen.

That case was easy compared to the fighting in the 1970s and early 1980s over the construction of the H-3 freeway between urban Honolulu and the windward side of O'ahu. I don't think I've ever seen such a fierce legal and political battle. Opponents of the freeway cited federal environmental laws, destruction of Hawaiian sites, you name it. To be blunt, I thought the state had done everything it was supposed to do, and that's how I generally ruled. But the Ninth Circuit, as was often its habit, reversed me. Then, one day—all of a sudden—Senator Dan Inouye made the whole thing moot. He pushed through a law that effectively exempts H-3 from most federal environmental regulations. My first thought was, "Why didn't he do that five years ago?"

I was trying to enforce the law as I read it, but, fundamentally, I thought the project should go through. The highway was going to be built somewhere, sometime, and all these objections raised the cost significantly. The opponents were being unnecessarily hardnosed. They made little effort to find a compromise. The same could be said of the state.

I do think the opponents had a point, though, about the proposal to put the freeway through Moanalua Valley. It's a beautiful place and they should have thought about alternatives a lot earlier. It might have been cheaper, but not going through Moanalua Valley—it ended up a valley over in Halawa—was probably an improvement.

I had another interesting case in the mid-1970s, when Governor George Ariyoshi challenged the U.S. Constitution in an effort, as he put it, to have Hawai'i "control our own destiny." The basic idea was to limit growth in Hawai'i.

The state was in turmoil over the post-statehood influx of people. Some felt the newcomers were overwhelming our social and political systems. So Ariyoshi took a bold step and announced in a state-of-the-state speech that he would, as some critics described it, "pull up the drawbridge" to protect what the governor frequently called "a special place." Ariyoshi declared his willingness to "put this state in direct confrontation with the present laws of this land, and possibly even the Constitution of the United States." Politically interesting, but legally not so good.

One element of Ariyoshi's plan was a residency requirement for government employment. Within a year, four newcomers who had been denied employment filed suit in federal court, and the case came before me.

I empathized with the feelings behind Ariyoshi's effort, but the issue in front of me was whether the law was constitutional. In fact, I wrote:

"Mark Twain once described the Hawaiian Islands as the 'loveliest fleet of islands that lies anchored in any ocean.' That feeling has certainly been shared by a large number of people from every racial, ethnic and cultural background. For over a thousand years, people have been traveling to Hawai'i and they have been staying in ever increasing numbers. As with almost all good things, which are not in limitless supply in this world, many of the 'haves do not wish to share their good fortune with the 'have nots.'" Clearly, their wish was not the law. The U.S. Supreme Court had previously declared that sort of thing unconstitutional under the Equal Protection Clause of the Fourteenth Amendment.

During my time on the bench, I've made friends with many in the media, and I've had a few run-ins as well. But I never took any of them personally.

My most memorable case involving the media became known as Fasi v. Borreca. Honolulu Mayor Frank Fasi became irritated for some reason with

Star-Bulletin reporter Richard Borreca and announced he was banning Borreca from his news conferences. Naturally, the paper objected. Fasi tried to defuse the situation by saying all the paper had to do was send another reporter. The paper didn't agree. Fasi then tried the ploy of saying he was simply holding "individual interviews on a group basis," which left him free to invite whomever he wanted into his inner sanctum. At least that's how he viewed it.

The paper sued in federal court and I got the case. It seemed an obvious violation of the First Amendment to me. I observed in my ruling: "One would have to be naive to believe that an individual reporter is solely responsible for the manner in which that reporter's news stories appear in print. Thus, Mayor Fasi's objections to Borreca's performance as a reporter can equally be taken as objections to the *Honolulu Star-Bulletin*'s approach to City Hall news." That's what made it unconstitutional.

I like to think I know a little about how newspapers work. I've had other newspaper cases, and, don't forget, I was a correspondent for the *Star-Bulletin* during my travels in high school! Besides, what Fasi tried to do was not even close. It was absolutely unconstitutional. When I would see Frank around town from time to time we never talked about the case.

Actually, I never had any real beef with Fasi. I guess he liked to fight with everybody—even me on one occasion. He got into an attack on me for some thing or another after I lost my race for governor. Hal Lewis, better known as J. Akuhead Pupule, invited both of us to appear on his popular morning radio show. So I went on and attacked Frank right back, but Aku had served his purpose, which was to boost ratings for his show. Later on, Frank and I became relatively friendly. That was even after I had to put one of his family members—his eldest son—back into prison for violating his probation after a drug conviction. Soon after that I ran into Frank downtown, where he was having coffee with his cronies, and I told him, "I'm sorry about your son, but there wasn't much I could do." And he simply said: "Oh, I understand."

To show you what a small town this is, when Fasi switched parties and became a Republican, my son and two other people formed a "Republicans for Frank Fasi" committee. I didn't participate. ❧

Chapter Twelve

Murder on the High Seas

Of all the criminal cases I handled as a federal judge, none came close to the publicity generated by the Palmyra murders case. It was a case made for the movies and, in fact, inspired a two-part mini-series on CBS television in 1991. It was also the subject of a book by well-known California lawyer Vincent Bugliosi, *And the Sea Will Tell*. I was kind of a bad guy in Bugliosi's book, but so be it.

The story begins in 1974, when an ex-convict named Buck Duane Walker and his girlfriend, Stephanie Stearns, got their hands on an old 30-foot sloop and fixed it up, although it was still in lousy shape. In June of that year, Walker pleaded guilty on the Mainland to one federal count of possessing the drug MDA with intent to sell. Before he could be sentenced he and Stearns set sail for Palmyra Island, a privately owned atoll about halfway between Hawai'i and Samoa. I already knew about the place because the Statehood Commission had sent me to talk to Congress about the legal status of Palmyra. The federal government wanted it, but there were people who had a land court title guaranteed by the territorial government of Hawai'i. That's what I went up to Washington to explain. I didn't get anywhere with Congress. Palmyra remained in private hands for years, but eventually it was taken over by the U.S. Fish and Wildlife Service in cooperation with the Nature Conservancy.

Walker and Stearns managed to find their way to Palmyra despite not much sailing experience and a barely seaworthy boat. There they met a well-to-do couple from San Diego named Malcolm and Eleanor Graham, who were aboard their yacht, a much nicer boat, named the *Sea Wind*.

No one will ever know exactly what happened between the two couples. What we do know—and there was plenty evidence at three trials I presided over to support it—is that something terrible happened to the Grahams, and that Walker and Stearns ended up with the Grahams' boat.

By October, Stearns and Walker were back in Honolulu with the *Sea Wind*, which had been repainted and given the name *Lokahi*. The new paint and new name didn't fool anyone, at least not folks in the Ala Wai Harbor yachting community, who recognized the *Sea Wind* and immediately notified the Coast Guard and the FBI. The authorities found Stearns' three dogs aboard *Sea Wind*, but no sign of her or Walker. Eventually the dogs began barking—"Arf! Arf! Arf!"—and Stearns ran from a nearby pier to put them below. That was her undoing. She was not a mean person. Walker would have thrown the dogs over a long time ago.

A Coast Guard officer managed to catch Stearns when she tried to run, but Walker escaped by jumping into the harbor and swimming away. He wasn't loose for long. About 10 days later he turned himself in to agents on the Big Island. At that point, all the authorities had on them were the yacht theft charges. There were no bodies and no evidence as to what happened to the Grahams. Walker claimed he found the Grahams' overturned dinghy on the beach and assumed they had drowned somewhere in the Palmyra lagoon. A jury quickly convicted them of theft. I sentenced Walker to a ten-year term in prison because of his previous record and an earlier prison escape. I gave Stearns a much shorter sentence, and the parole board released her after only seven months. That made sense to me because I didn't think she was really a bad person. She was kind of a free spirit, and Buck was feeding her marijuana. That's what got her into trouble. She didn't show any propensity for violence. After Stearns got out of prison, she sent me a Christmas card! I've had it in my desk all of these years.

Walker was different. He was good-looking and had a brain, but he didn't use it for legal means. He was downright mean. He was also fearless. Imagine getting a broken-down sloop and heading for a tiny spot in the South Pacific without any knowledge of navigation—and managing to find the place.

When the theft trial ended, I thought I was done with those two, but then something happened. In January 1981, a woman named Sharon Jordan was walking on the beach on Palmyra and found what appeared to be human bones, including a skull. She picked up the skull and took it back to her husband. Imagine that: "Hi, honey, I found a skull."

She was suspicious because everyone in the yachting crowd knew about the disappearance of the Grahams. Later, she testified at the murder trial.

The FBI took custody of the bones and a metal container found nearby. It was determined by dental records that they had what was left of Mrs. Graham. They weren't able to figure out the time or cause of death, but they could tell that her body had been dismembered. Within a month, a federal grand jury indicted both Stearns and Walker on murder charges. She turned herself in but he remained loose for months, until he was betrayed in Arizona by an associate who apparently had become a government informant.

I was assigned the case, and, before long, the defense asked for a change of venue. I transferred the case to San Francisco because the details were too well known in Hawai'i. There wasn't anybody in Hawai'i old enough to be on a jury who wouldn't have read or heard a lot about it.

By the way, I'd like to straighten out a myth that has developed around my decision to move the case to San Francisco. Both my wife and I enjoy opera, and some people said I switched the case so we could go to the opera. That's a stupid statement. If the defense had not asked for it, I wouldn't have moved the trial. If my wife went to the opera, I slept at night to get my strength for the next day.

It was during the 1982 murder trial that Bugliosi got involved as one of Stearns' attorneys. Bugliosi was well known. After successfully prosecuting the original Charles Manson-Tate-LaBianca murder cases, he had written a bestseller about the cases, *Helter Skelter*. He joined the Stearns defense team and cut an imposing figure in court. I suspected that he had cut a book and movie deal with Stearns and her family. That's something that always bothered me. That would have been unethical, because of the conflict between the client's interests and the lawyer's desire to have a great story to tell.

Bugliosi was convinced all along that Buck, who was eventually convicted, was a murderer, and I thought so, too. Walker knew that the boat they sailed down to Palmyra would never survive another trip. They needed a different vessel and he killed the Grahams to get it. No question in my mind.

In the murder trial for Walker, one of the best witnesses I ever heard was the coroner from San Francisco. He had an explanation for why Eleanor Graham's body eventually showed up and her husband's didn't. He pointed out that, when a body deteriorates, it lets off a lot of gas. If Eleanor's body had been underwater in a sealed container, the gases would have eventually caused the container to float to the surface and the lid to pop off. He said if they ever find a submerged container with Malcolm Graham's remains, there will probably be holes in it to let the gases escape.

Did that explain why one body was found and one wasn't? It made sense to the jury and that's what matters. It's always up to the jury.

But I don't doubt Walker killed them both.

Postscript: Sam King the Wizard
During jury selection at one of the Palmyra trials, I accidentally attracted worldwide news coverage. There had been a lot of bad weather in California at the time of that trial, so people weren't showing up for jury duty. As a joke, I issued a court order: "I hereby order that it cease raining by Tuesday." Well, guess what? It stopped raining on Tuesday. In fact, California went on to

suffer a long drought. Five years later, when I was again sitting on a case in California, I got a tongue-in-cheek request from an official with the Santa Clara Water District asking me to rescind my order, so I did: "I hereby rescind my order of February 18, 1986, and order that rain shall fall in California beginning February 27, 1991." Actually, my secretary, Rebecca Berry, had checked the weather reports and saw that rain was predicted for February 27. That's why she and I weren't exactly shocked when the state was hit by heavy rainstorms that day.

Even so, the word got out to reporters from the *Los Angeles Times*, *San Francisco Examiner* and *Honolulu Star-Bulletin* about my "orders" that Mother Nature had obeyed. Before long, reporters from around the world were also calling. The story even made it into Ripley's "Believe It or Not!" The Water District sent me a Certificate of Appreciation printed in several colors.

Whenever people ask me about this, I say that it shows the awesome power of the federal courts. ❧

Chapter Thirteen

KING THE LIBERAL

I've always been a Republican, but some say I have a liberal streak. I'd rather think of myself as a pragmatist who sees the human dimension of things.

Take abortion, for instance. In my opinion, there shouldn't be any law at all. It's a private matter. That was the position taken by Jack Burns when he was governor, and I agree with it.

The same goes for marriage of almost any kind. The government shouldn't be in that business, except for laws such as you cannot marry your own sister. In the old days, there was no statute that said who could get married. My attitude is: If you say you are married, you are married. That includes same-sex couples. If two people want to be married, I say, "Why not?"

I never enjoyed criminal trials, particularly sentencing. Throughout my career, I've always had trouble sending people to prisons. Convicts learn all the tricks of the trade there, and the ones that happen to be young and not tough enough get abused. Terrible. No wonder most people come out of prison worse than when they went in.

Yet for many years as a federal judge—before I achieved senior status and stopped taking criminal cases—I had no choice but to send many people to prison for long stretches of time. This is due to federal mandatory sentencing guidelines, which were a feel-good effort by politicians to appear tough on crime. Many people think the problem lies with bleeding heart, soft–headed liberal judges who pass out light sentences to career criminals or for violent crimes.

"What we need," they say, "is mandatory minimum sentences and faster and surer punishment."

That makes for good rhetoric, but it's based on three false assumptions: that most law violators are caught, charged with and convicted of the crimes they committed, that career and violent criminals do not end up in prison and that severe sentences deter crime. None of this is true. Mandatory sentencing made little sense to me, or to many of my fellow judges who had to face criminal defendants almost every day. Each defendant had a different story.

Not that long ago, prisons also served as warehouses for mentally sick people. I've always believed if someone is that way, they should get treatment—not punishment—even if they commit serious crimes. This isn't an idea I came to after becoming a judge. It dates back to my days as an attorney for the Republicans in the Territorial Legislature. In that capacity, I drafted one of the first laws governing the care of mentally ill people who come to the attention of the police. It said the police couldn't just throw them in jail; instead, they had to take them to the doctor. I thought that approach made a lot of sense, but the U.S. Supreme Court eventually thought otherwise. So, later, when I became a federal judge, I had to declare my own law unconstitutional.

That was in the 1970s, when there was a big debate, both in Hawai'i and across the nation, over the proper way to handle people with mental illnesses. Hawai'i had moved away from giving the police free rein, but they were still incarcerating people with mental-health, drug-addiction or alcoholism problems. Maybe not in prison, but there was mandatory confinement of some kind.

In two decisions involving a woman named Sharon Suzuki, I declared unconstitutional part of the state mental-health law I had earlier drafted. The two decisions, in 1976 and 1977, helped lay down the guidelines for involuntary civil commitments for the mentally ill and later became the subject of frequent seminars on how to treat the mentally ill: "I believe the requirements of substantive due process are met only when an individual is found to be dangerous to himself or to others, and thus hold that dangerousness to property is not a constitutional basis for commitment in an emergency or nonemergency situation." As I described it privately, "If a guy is caught peeing on the side of the building, that doesn't mean the government can put him away."

And as long as I can recall, I've opposed the death penalty, which is a cruel and wasteful process. The government just has no business killing people, even if they deserve to die. Part of that comes from my dad. He had a chance to put his convictions into action in the case of James Majors and John Palakiko. They escaped from an O'ahu Prison work gang and found themselves in upper Nu'uanu, where they came across the home of Therese Wilder. She was about sixty-seven at the time, I think. They supposedly were attracted to her house by the smell of cooking. They broke in and strangled her—and there was evidence that a rape had also occurred, or at least was attempted. It was a heinous crime.

These two were sentenced to death by hanging and were only minutes from the gallows when the outgoing governor, Oren Long, stayed their execution. That bought them some time. Then the legal wrangling began. My father succeeded Long as appointed governor. So Harriet Bouslog, who had a strong reputation as a liberal and civil rights supporter, came to me and asked a favor. Bouslog wasn't afraid to go up against authority—she fought for union rights for years—and she was a strong opponent of the death penalty.

We weren't exactly on the same side of the political fence, but she knew I had my father's ear.

"What's the best way to approach your father and what is the best way to convince him not to apply the death penalty?" she asked.

I counseled patience. I said: "Just leave him alone." And, sure enough, two or three months later, he commuted their sentences to life in prison. That was in 1954. By 1957, the Legislature had outlawed the death penalty in Hawai'i. So, if my father had not acted, Majors and Palakiko would have been the last two people executed in the Islands.

As an aside, Governor Burns pardoned the two in 1962. I never understood that. Palakiko found his way back to prison for parole violation. I don't know what happened to Majors.

The closest I came to a death-penalty case was as a visiting judge in Arizona, assigned to hear a federal challenge to a death sentence. Two guys had used their wives and children as decoys, and they put their victims in sacks and threw them into the water, alive. The prosecutors were furious with me when I granted a stay of execution.

In a case like that, you're of two minds, but a stay was legally warranted. My ruling gave one of them a little more time. They were both finally executed later on.

People don't always understand the difference between the law and common sense. And I'm the first to admit, the law does not always allow for common sense. Take the O.J. Simpson murder trial. People always ask me: "Did O.J. do it?" My response is that they are asking the wrong question. The right question is: "Did O.J. have a fair trial?"

Part of the problem, as I see it, is that we rely too much on government to settle issues that should be handled another way. I remember reading a *New York Times* article by Thomas Ehrlich, arguing that the United States has too many laws. I couldn't agree more. Here's what I said about that in a 1976 speech: "We rely on law too heavily as an instrument of social change (or to prevent social change); and we rely too much on courts, legislatures and administrative agencies to resolve our woes (and to perpetuate the other fellow's woes)." That may sound strange coming from a judge, but I believe it.

By and large, crime is a natural part of the human condition. If you want to know how people live, and what they believe, just look at the criminal laws. For instance, the Hawaiians once had a law making it illegal to pray somebody to death. We don't make it a crime to do something nobody does anyway.

We can structure situations to reduce the temptations leading a person into antisocial behavior, but we cannot eliminate such conduct. It's not even clear how much conflict a given society should encourage or could tolerate. Too much conflict leads to disintegration, and too little conflict leads to stagnation. No one is sure where the middle ground lies. I suppose that's what ensures plenty of work for people like me.

When I first became a federal judge in 1972, it was close to paradise. Working conditions were pleasant, and I didn't have to think about politics. The issues brought before the court were worth thinking about, and there was a fair amount of camaraderie among district judges around the country, since there were only about 275 in all, including retired judges. That led to a certain amount of undemocratic satisfaction in being a member of an exclusive club. And the power a federal judge could wield was awesome.

But things began to change. A flurry of new laws, environmental and otherwise, liberalized rules of procedure and the growth of multistate class-action lawsuits combined to open the federal courts to a whole new category of activity. And lawyers became clever at finding ways to bring cases that should have been in state court into the federal arena. What had been a dream was becoming a nightmare.

I used to believe that a person who had been convicted of a crime at the trial level was thereupon presumed to be guilty. But now it seems that the convicted criminal is still presumed to be innocent until an appellate court has rejected his appeal, which usually happens, and then the Supreme Court denies certiorari, which almost always happens. Meanwhile, the convicted criminal is typically free on bail, and, when his conviction is finally affirmed two or three years later, he can usually plead for a reduced sentence by showing he's led a blameless life since his arrest. This means the trial judge is dragged through the sentencing procedure twice, with increased emotional strain for everyone concerned.

I've enjoyed being a judge, but I sometimes wonder what I've accomplished. The law is a marvelous thing, but we don't get very far with statutes that try to alter human nature. ❧

Chapter Fourteen

Bishop Estate and Broken Trust

I never wanted to be a Bishop Estate trustee. People assumed I did because my father was a trustee for the two years before his death in 1959. I was part of a lawsuit against the Hawai'i Supreme Court over the selection of a trustee, and I was co-signer on the 1997 essay "Broken Trust," which helped fuel badly needed changes in the way the estate was run. But that kind of job just isn't my style. Being a federal judge is more fun. And I get a salary until I die, or at least as long as I am on "good behavior." I could have made more money during my lifetime, but you have to ask yourself, "What's money?" My mother always said, "Money's nothing."

But not everybody feels that way. Bishop Estate started being treated like a cookie jar by politicians in the 1980s when the previously land-rich, cash-poor trust came into a great deal of money. Ironically, I had something to do with that. In 1979, based on the reasoning of state Circuit Court Judge Masato Doi's opinion, I upheld a law that let the state force the owners of leased land to sell it to the individual homeowners on that land. The buyers had to pay fair value, but that didn't make this an easy case from a legal standpoint. It just seemed wrong—at first blush anyway—to force landowners to sell their land to private parties, even if the prices were high. The resulting sale of Bishop Estate holdings made the estate a bit less land-rich, and a lot less cash-poor.

Mandatory leasehold conversion—that's what people called the state law—was more than just a legal issue. It was a political issue, because it was a cornerstone of the Democratic Party's platform and opposed by the Republicans—or at least the ones that weren't leaseholders wanting to buy the land under their homes. It was also a social issue, because Bishop Estate was and still is the largest private landowner in the state, by far. I thought mandatory conversion was well within the state's police powers. I explained in my legal opinion, "The legislature had the right to conclude that Hawai'i's system of landholding was injurious to the social and economic health of the community."

This was a classic case of how a person's background or understanding of the local situation can affect his decision. I had to admit it was impossible for me not to be aware of what, as I said in my ruling, was a "rather uncommon system of land holding" in Hawai'i. From my perspective, living in Hawai'i, I could easily see how the Legislature concluded that leasehold conversion was good for society here. Someone from the Mainland wouldn't necessarily see it that way. And many Hawaiians also disagreed. They felt it was improper for the state to take what they considered their land and sell it to homeowners who were mostly non-Hawaiians. They would show up in large numbers at rallies, wearing T-shirts reading, THOU SHALT NOT STEAL.

All I was doing, essentially, was deferring to the wisdom of the state Legislature. To rule the other way would overturn the thinking of the people elected to make policy for Hawai'i. Even so, it seems strange to some that a former Republican candidate for governor would be the one to uphold the heart of the Democrats' political agenda.

The controversy didn't actually end with my decision. The Ninth Circuit Court up on the Mainland reversed me, using phrases like "majoritarian tyranny" to describe the law that I had upheld. But then the U.S. Supreme Court reversed *them*—as it often did—upholding my decision, eight-zip. The ninth justice, Thurgood Marshall, recused himself since he was married to a Hawai'i girl.

I was not surprised when the Ninth Circuit reversed me, nor when the Supreme Court reversed the Ninth Circuit. I once asked a lawyer in my courtroom, "Do you remember that case we had a year ago or so?" "Yes," he replied. "Well, the Ninth Circuit just affirmed my decision," I said. And then, before he could say anything else, I added, "but I still think I'm right!"

I had tangled with Bishop Estate trustees and their political associates years earlier, when the justices appointed former city councilman and Jack Burns' protégé Matsy Takabuki to the estate's board in 1971. The Hawaiians were furious because Takabuki was Japanese, not Hawaiian. The bells at Kawaiaha'o Church rang loudly and there were big marches on Bishop Estate headquarters. Revolution was in the air.

I was still in private practice at that time, and I agreed to represent Kamehameha Schools alumni, parents and students, who were questioning the justices' involvement in the trustee-selection process. They had lost at the trial level and I took the case on appeal. I wasn't so much interested in the racial angle. But I cared a great deal that the justices had done what Burns told them to do. It was bound to politicize the trust and have a corrupting effect on our judiciary.

The justices pushed politics to the breaking point twelve years later when they appointed Chief Justice Richardson to be a Bishop Estate trustee. Imagine that! The justices looked around the room and discovered that one of them was the best, most qualified person in the state to appoint to a job that would more than quadruple his salary. They even gave him an extra two years past the normal retirement date as a trustee. It was shocking but not really a big surprise. And the political manipulation didn't stop there. Not content with just a former chief justice on the Bishop Estate board, the justices added a Senate president, a House speaker and a chairman of the Judicial Selection Commission.

The process was circular: Seven of the nine members of the Judicial Selection Commission were appointed by the chief justice, House speaker, Senate president and governor, and to become a Supreme Court justice you had to get the Judicial Selection Commission to put you on a short list of candidates. Someone once asked me if these connections were just coincidences or could be attributed to political maneuvering. I told him, "If it quacks like a duck, walks like a duck, and lays duck eggs—it's a duck!"

In the earlier Takabuki case, everyone knew that the justices had to disqualify themselves from deciding the case. After all, they were the ones who had made the appointment that my clients were questioning. But the replacements were selected by Chief Justice Richardson himself, though I argued that the replacement justices should be selected randomly by lot from the names of every circuit court judge. They were hardly independent. I was not surprised when they ruled in favor of the justices.

Takabuki was great with finances, but not necessarily great for a charitable institution. He pushed the estate to invest its newfound wealth in high-flying Mainland investments. A substantial stake in Goldman Sachs worked out financially, but many others did not. More important, the trustees started treating Princess Pauahi's trust like their own investment company. That's how the IRS described all the wheeling and self-dealing in the 1990s, and it almost cost the estate its tax exemption.

The money was flowing and they got carried away. But I continue to think that the things the trust stands for and the things it accomplished in the way of education and support for Hawaiians has been good. In fact, until the board became full of people who saw it as an opportunity to line their own pockets, I think the Bishop Estate did considerable good.

By then I was convinced that two problems needed to be fixed. The first was the political nonsense of having the justices select trustees. Granted, that is what the will of Mrs. Bishop stipulated, but times were different back then. When she wrote her will, the Supreme Court handled everything, including probate, and they were loyal to her. In effect, she was saying, "My servants will name the trustees."

By the 1980s and 1990s, members of the Hawai'i Supreme Court

Sam chats with Honolulu Mayor Frank F. Fasi (center), and Hawaiʻi Governor John A. Burns.

Top: Sam takes his campaign on the road during his unsuccessful run for governor in 1970.

Bottom: At a political rally with Randolph Crossley (left), a businessman and politician with whom he often crossed swords.

Hebden Porteus congratulates Sam on his victory in the 1970 gubernatorial primary.

Sam stands outside his state courtroom in 1965 (top) and later occupies his book-filled office in the Prince Kūhiō Federal Building.

*A master of the Japanese board game Go, Sam was also an avid chess player who,
on occasion, even kept a game going while in court.*

Sam shares a light moment ca. 1970s with longtime colleague and fellow federal judge Martin Pence.
Left to right: Pence, King, First Lady Jean Ariyoshi, Gov. George Ariyoshi, State Supreme Court
Justice Herman Lum and Hawai'i State Bar Association President David Fairbanks.

Sam waves as he leads his fellow justices out of federal court after a program, held shortly before
his death, honoring his contributions. "It's not the mind," he observed, "it's the legs!"

*The authors of the original "Broken Trust" essay (left to right): Walter Heen, Sam King,
Gladys Brandt, Monsignor Charles Kekumano and Randy Roth.*

Sam celebrates with a cookie at his retirement party, Prince Kūhiō Federal Building, 2010.

were political appointees—they lacked jurisdiction over probate matters—and Bishop Estate had a constant parade of disputes being decided by the state courts, including the Supreme Court, which had appointed them in the first place. A classic conflict of interests.

The second obvious problem was the money. Each trustee was taking $800,000-$900,000 a year in fees, plus a bunch of extras. Trust experts said the fees were way out of line and that serious breaches of trust were apparent. The trustees were getting away with it because of the justices' too-close involvement, as well as the knee-jerk support of Hawaiian groups. The rest of the community was told, in effect, to butt out.

What's wrong with a little exciting investment and a big trustee paycheck when there's a lot of money washing around? It's easy to forget in all this drama that Bishop Estate was founded with the express purpose of aiding and educating Native Hawaiian children, not of enriching itself or its trustees. What made change possible was "The March" of May 1997. After years of defending the trustees against outsiders, the Kamehameha School 'ohana publicly criticized the trustees. Hawaiians had marched on behalf of the Bishop Estate before. But it was mostly in an effort to keep the larger community out of their affairs. That was the case with *Takabuki*. Many felt their *kuleana* was being meddled with. Over the years, when criticism of the Estate came up, their response was, in effect, "we'll handle it ourselves." This was different.

The marchers were particularly troubled by the antics of trustee Lokelani Lindsay, a former state education administrator from Maui who felt she knew best how to run the school and who some said was out to get rid of its beloved president, Michael Chun. So the 'ohana gathered at the Royal Mausoleum in Nu'uanu and marched through downtown Honolulu to estate headquarters on King and South Streets. It was a remarkable display of courage, because the trustees were known to play rough. Photographers hired by the trustees were there, taking pictures of all the marchers so lawyers from a big downtown firm could prepare a file on each one.

The attorney for the marchers, Beadie Kanahele Dawson, later charged in court that the trustees had demoralized and gutted the educational core of the campus and its students by focusing on accumulating profits and letting Lindsay—who the other trustees had named "lead trustee" for education—impose her own warped ideas of what the school should be. Dawson wrote, "This case (also) concerns the estimated 40,000 children, many now grown to adulthood, who have been denied a Kamehameha education solely because Trustees have chosen deliberately or in inexcusable ignorance, to accumulate funds instead of furthering and expanding the Trust's benefit to more children."

I was watching this from a distance with growing concern. Then UH law professor Randy Roth, an expert on taxes and trust law, came to me with a draft of something that was highly critical of the trustees and the justices who selected those trustees. It was a long essay—it eventually became known as "Broken Trust"—and he asked if I would consider joining him. I had been a guest on his radio program, and we hit it off pretty well. After that we would occasionally meet and talk about all sorts of things, so he knew about my interest in Bishop Estate, which had nothing to do with Bishop Estate as such, but about the corruption of the judiciary.

I told Randy I was willing to be a co-author if it was okay with my wife. Randy later said he thought I was kidding about needing Annie's permission. I was absolutely 100-percent serious, but I knew she would say yes. Annie has been fully in favor of all my big decisions, except when I ran for office. I'll never do that again.

As expected, Annie's answer was, "Yes!" I relayed that to Randy and added some advice: "If it's just the two of us, it's not going to go anywhere. They're going to throw rocks. No one is going to pay attention to the issues."

After all, the *haoles*—newspapers and so forth—had criticized the trustees before. Nothing had happened. The trustees would call up the newspaper editors and threaten all kinds of economic disaster. Then they would round up the Kamehameha *'ohana* and have them picket the Legislature and all that kind of thing. In this case, if they hadn't already marched, the *'ohana* would have been organized by the trustees to come down and say, "Impeach Judge King" and that sort of stuff.

I told Randy, "Always remember that we're in this to help the *'ohana*; we're not the prime movers." The *'ohana* [Nā Pua O Keali'i Pauahi, the Kamehameha organization of parents, students and alumni] were being pushed around by big lawyers and so we were able to help them. If we weren't supporting the *'ohana*, rather than attacking the estate, I didn't want anything to do with it. I also told him we needed to beef up our ranks. Gladys Brandt, a former Kamehameha Schools principal, immediately came to mind. She was a widely respected community leader, and tough—boy, was she tough. No way would she waver when the going got rough.

I later learned that Gladys herself had a bit of an axe to grind with the justices. Several years earlier, she had been appointed by Chief Justice Ronald Moon to chair a blue-ribbon committee whose job was to make a short list of candidates for the next Bishop Estate trustee opening. Moon promised the committee that the justices would select someone from their list. He said this process would eliminate the politics. No chance. Moon and the other justices ignored the committee's list and instead named Gerard Jervis, a buddy of then-Governor Waihee, who also just happened to chair the Judicial Selection Committee at key times. Gladys said the betrayal made her feel "used and abused," so she and the others renamed themselves the "Black and Blue" Committee.

Randy went to Gladys's place and asked her to read the essay. She did so and then said to Randy, "You say Sam King is with you on this?" When Randy said that I was, Gladys said, "Then count me in."

Gladys understood what we were up against. To strengthen our team she suggested that we recruit Monsignor Charles Kekumano. He was head trustee of the Queen Liliʻuokalani Children's Trust, and he had a habit of sticking his nose into Hawaiian affairs when there was a problem. He had also served with Gladys on the "Black and Blue" Committee. The two of them had been working together on education issues, going up to the Kapālama campus, talking with teachers and administrators. Gladys had even taken trustee Lindsay to lunch and tried to talk some sense into her, but that was like talking to a stone wall, according to Gladys.

Then Randy suggested that we invite retired state Judge Walter Heen to join us. I had long respected and thought highly of Walter, and I liked that he was a staunch Democrat. After all, we didn't want anyone thinking that our essay had anything to do with partisan politics.

The bad guys in this story were undeniably all Democrats, which would have stopped just about anyone in Walter's shoes, but it didn't stop him. Walter's got more smarts and guts than just about anyone I know. And, like me, he was convinced that trustee selection was corrupting the judiciary.

I said, "That's great! We've got a Democrat, a Republican, a Kamehameha principal, a trust lawyer and a Catholic cleric." But there was something about this group that was sort of funny: In her will, Princess Pauahi required that her trustees and teachers always be "members of the Protestant religion," and some people in those days viewed that as code for "they can't be Catholics." Of the five "Broken Trust" authors, I think I was the only non-Catholic!

I suppose it was no accident that four of us were *kūpuna*. The older you get, the less you care what other people think. In fact, the trustees later tried to discredit our work by saying we were "old and senile." When Gladys heard that, she said someone ought to explain to them that old and senile is the most dangerous kind.

I'm the first to acknowledge that few federal judges would intentionally put themselves at the center of the kind of controversy our essay unleashed. A lot of people think judges should keep their noses out of controversy, except in the courtroom. But Randy got an opinion from a professor at the law school, saying it was okay for me to be a co-author, and I got another one from a retired ethics professor.

My friend and fellow Judge Martin Pence was concerned. "You shouldn't be out in public that way," he said. And he didn't say "maybe" you shouldn't do that, he said, "*You shouldn't do that!*" So I said, "Thank you for your advice," and went ahead. But, as I said before, a judge is obligated to speak out from time to time.

I found out later that the trustees paid a big downtown law firm a lot of money to find a legal or ethical argument against my involvement. They wanted to change the conversation from whether they were ripping off the trust to whether I had done something wrong. That was predictable. They eventually decided they couldn't do it, but someone had their guns out for me.

The five of us—we called ourselves Pauahi's gang—would get together and work on the essay: polish and so forth. We worked well together and had a lot of fun. Gladys and Monsignor were always cracking jokes and kidding each other. Make no mistake, though, we were dead serious about the subject matter of our essay and the need to take action: It was common knowledge at the time that you didn't get on the court unless you would take a suggestion as to who should be a Bishop Estate trustee. That wasn't good for the Bishop Estate, and it wasn't good for the state judiciary, either. Gladys, Monsignor, Randy and especially Walter agreed that the justices had no business selecting trustees, and that it was corrupting the judiciary and politicizing the estate.

We knew the essay was controversial, but fortunately the *Star-Bulletin* published it in its entirety the day after we gave it to them.

One of my fondest memories from those days was attending a party the Monsignor gave for Gladys on her ninety-first birthday, which was shortly after the *Star-Bulletin* published our essay. Monsignor made a nice toast and then put a beautiful lei around Gladys' neck and gave her a little kiss on the cheek. To lighten the moment, Gladys said, "Well, will you look at that! After ninety-one years I finally get a kiss from the monsignor." With a twinkle in his eye, Monsignor said, "Kind of makes you wonder what she'll get next year, doesn't it."

In the end, the trustees were removed under pressure from the Internal Revenue Service and others, and the Supreme Court justices got out of the business of appointing trustees, which was essentially what I argued should have happened years before in the Takabuki case. I guess these things take time. ❧

Chapter Fifteen

EULOGY

On December 7, 2010, at age ninety-four, Judge Samuel King suffered a fall in his Honolulu apartment and died of the resulting injuries. In Chicago, where King often heard cases as a visiting judge, Chief Judge James Holderman called his court to order the next day with a tribute to King, in which he spoke movingly about his love for "a great man." In Hawai'i, King's funeral services—a combination of Hawaiian traditional ritual and Episcopalian liturgy—were attended by many of Hawai'i's most prominent business, political and legal leaders, Republicans and Democrats alike, as well as ordinary citizens whose lives he had touched in some way. The eulogy was delivered by UH law professor Randy Roth, a co-author of the "Broken Trust" essay and book. Following are excerpts from that eulogy.

Abraham Lincoln said, "Nearly all men can stand adversity, but if you want to test a man's character, give him power." Samuel Pailthorpe King was the most powerful man I've ever known. His power derived from extraordinary intelligence, eloquence, charisma and wit, not to mention thirty-eight years as a federal judge. Yet the legacy he leaves is not about power. It's about character.

Sam genuinely cared about others and treated everyone with respect and aloha. He did not hesitate to stand up to injustice. He managed to stay humble throughout a lifetime of personal successes. And he did it all with humor and grace while being the most loving husband, father, grandfather and friend imaginable.

Sam was my role model, mentor and best friend. And I'm not alone. I've met many others who have said the same thing.

Sam and I first met about fifteen years ago when I asked him to be a guest on a call-in radio show that I hosted. The scheduled topic was O.J. Simpson's acquittal on charges of first-degree murder. Not many judges would engage in a public conversation like that, but Sam said he'd do it, if it was okay with his wife, Anne. At the time, I thought he was kidding about needing Anne's permission.

My first question during the live broadcast was whether Sam thought O.J. had done it. His response was that I had asked the wrong question. He said the right question was whether the trial was fair. I enjoyed and learned more from that interview than from any other.

Sam had similar control over his courtroom, which was one reason lawyers respected him so much. One practicing lawyer spoke for many in describing Sam as "born to judge," and as providing "predictable fairness."

There was also a healthy dose of humor in Sam's courtroom. One day there was a case involving eight exceptionally large reputed gangsters. Prospective jurors were coming up with one reason after another not to serve. When a woman said she would be willing to do her duty, but that she was about to move to Maui, Sam responded, "Oh, well, here today, gone to Maui." The prospective jurors had a good laugh and the newspapers had a headline that eventually ended up on T-shirts. Sam later explained: "I didn't invent the expression. I just used it to ease the tension." It worked perfectly: He was able to assemble a jury.

Sam never for a moment considered that his duties as a judge ended when he left the courtroom. He once commented that the whole purpose of government, besides maintaining public safety, is to protect the underprivileged from the privileged. At a different time, he told a reporter, "Every judge has an obligation: If you see something wrong in the community, you speak out against it."

Sam made a lifelong habit of standing up to injustice and abuses of power. One example is from the late 1940s, before he became a judge: The founders of the local chapters of the League of Woman Voters and American Civil Liberties Union, Alan and Marion Saunders, were being singled out for their "un-American" activities. To Sam it looked like a witch hunt. So he called the financially strapped couple to ask if they had a lawyer. When they said "No," he responded, "Well, you do now."

In 1997, I asked Sam if he would be willing to provide hands-on help with a public critique of the sitting Bishop Estate trustees. A federal judge's personal involvement in such an effort would itself be highly controversial. Once again Sam said yes—if it was okay with Anne.

Sam set the tone and direction of that effort, just as he had done when I interviewed him on the radio. He recognized that it would take more than two voices to succeed, but there was a potential problem: each of the essay's other eventual authors—Gladys Brandt, Monsignor Kekumano, and Walter Heen—also had good reasons not to get involved. But when Gladys saw the first draft of the essay she had only one question: "You say Sam King is with you on this?" I confirmed that he was, and she said, "Then count me in."

As the group's reporter, I did my best to put our collaborative thoughts into writing, and then Sam and the others commented. Sam liked brevity. He wrote on one of my drafts, "There's more here than I ever wanted to know."

After the essay appeared and evidence of additional fiduciary abuse came to light, a reporter met with Sam and me to talk about the latest revelation of trustee misconduct. Sam nodded in my direction, so I proceeded to provide what I probably thought was a brilliant lecture on fiduciaries and fiduciary duties, but the reporter looked confused. Then Sam added, "I don't think those trustees know how to *spell* 'fiduciary'," and the light went on.

Working with Sam for five years on the *Broken Trust* book was fun, and it gave me an opportunity to spend time with his three children: Sam Jr., Louise and Becky, and to hear Sam provide updates on the adventures and accomplishments of his six grandchildren: Chris, Sam, Sara, Charlotte, Anne and Nawa. Sam's family has a treasure trove of amazing memories, including a very low-budget, eye-opening trip around the world during the children's formative years. The stay in India impressed on them how much they had been given, and how much they had to give.

The King children once assembled a booklet on their parents' wit and wisdom. Here are several examples of things their father would often say to them, that—because of the surrounding circumstances—never failed to produce smiles and insights:

"If you don't want to do something, one reason is as good as another."

"If a man says his word is as good as his bond, get his bond."

"Our suspicions of others are based on our knowledge of ourselves."

"Laws are created for people; people aren't created for laws."

And finally: "Everything I say is either interesting or original—the part that's interesting isn't original and the part that's original isn't interesting."

Humor was a big part of the King household. I recall asking Sam the secret of his long, happy marriage. He stressed to me the importance of saying to my wife, as often as possible, those three magic words: "Let's … eat … out."

From his family and longtime friends, I learned that Sam had *ali'i* ancestors on both sides of his family tree. His *haole* ancestors included one who was made governor of O'ahu by Kamehameha I, and a sea captain who had set out on his own from the Donegal area of Scotland when he was fourteen years old.

Sam was fiercely proud of his Hawaiian roots, but he actually was born in China while his father was serving as the captain of a U.S. Navy gunboat. Sam later described his stay in the country of his birth as just long enough to learn how to cry in Chinese.

Sam lost an eye in an accident when he was six years old, but he never raised the subject. I once asked him what it had been like to lose an eye as a young boy. He shrugged and said, "You only need one, you know."

Sam attended Central Grammar School and then Punahou on a scholarship, where he was the student body president, one of the state's top milers, captain of the rifle team and a national-caliber orator. His speech-making skills won him a trip to Europe. During that trip he wrote a regular column for the *Honolulu Star-Bulletin*, called, "To Europe with Sam King." He was seventeen years old, and already a Renaissance man.

Sam had scholarship offers from both Harvard and Yale and chose the latter for both undergraduate and law studies, graduating with honors in 1940. He then earned his way back home by working on a freighter, spending six hours a day steering the vessel, and the rest of his time studying for the bar exam.

After Pearl Harbor was bombed, he became an officer in Naval Intelligence and was stationed in New Orleans because of his fluency in French. Sam wanted to get closer to the action, so he applied for the Navy's Japanese-language program. Anne also had applied for that program, in her case immediately upon graduating Phi Beta Kappa from Smith, where she majored in Greek.

It didn't take Sam long to make up his mind about Anne: Two weeks after their first date, he proposed. Anne responded with a Japanese word that expresses great surprise, and said that she didn't approve of wartime marriages. "But that's the only kind there is in wartime!" pleaded Sam. Anne thought about that for a moment, and then told him to ask her again in three days. Three days later he asked again, and this time Anne said yes.

When Leslie Wilcox interviewed Sam as part of her "Long Story Short" series, she asked what it was about Anne that attracted Sam. He said Anne was obviously intelligent, and then, with a twinkle in his eye, he added, "and she looked good—coming and going."

After the bombing of Hiroshima, Sam received orders to leave for Japan immediately. Once there, he toured the rubble in Hiroshima serving as a translator. He then served on board a minesweeper in Tokyo Bay, helping Allied forces locate and collect mines. Talking about it years later, Sam made it sound like just another day at the office: "Translating mine charts wasn't too hard … [I just had to] identify the area, and then the distance and the speed … [I]t was all in Japanese, but it was very simple Japanese."

After the war ended, Sam practiced law for a dozen years before being appointed a state judge. When Senator Hiram Fong asked him in 1972 if he was interested in being appointed to the federal bench, Sam responded, "Let me put it this way—*YES!*"

Sam was a humble man who seemed to give little thought to material possessions. For decades while serving as a federal judge, he drove an old Volkswagen bug. There was one form of material possession, however, that Sam loved—and that was his books. According to Doug Ushijima, "To know Judge King one need only have seen him as we law clerks did every day at his desk, surrounded by his personal library of some 6,000 books. Not law books (he kept those with the clerks), but American and world history, biography, politics, Polynesia, science, philosophy, mystery, humor. He often said—tongue-in-cheek, but with truth—that he could never retire because he needed someplace to keep his books."

Sometimes Sam's ability to do things seemed almost otherworldly. For example, he once ordered it to rain—and it did! The story began five years earlier when he was a visiting judge in California, and downpours had prevented jurors from making it to the courtroom. So Sam decreed from the bench, "I hereby order that it cease raining." The rain stopped later that day. In fact, that happened to be the beginning of a statewide drought. Five years later, when the director of the Santa Clara Water District heard that Sam happened to be presiding over another case in California, he wrote a letter asking Sam to rescind the earlier decree. Sam's secretary, Rebecca (who, incidentally, worked for him for fifty-five years) showed Sam both the letter and an extended weather report predicting rain. So Sam issued a formal decree, ordering the rain to fall. Sure enough, a fierce rainstorm commenced the next day and continued for days. Sam explained to reporters that these events were "proof positive that we are a nation governed by laws."

A year or so ago Sam and I talked about the important things in our lives. I asked what he considered the meaning of life, and he said, "Family." Then I asked what had been his proudest moment over the course of his entire lifetime, and he said, "Marrying Anne." Finally, I asked him how I could become wise, like him. He just smiled and said, "Let's go have lunch."

All of us gathered today, and especially Sam's family, are feeling a great loss—an almost unbearable loss. But I can't help thinking that Sam would want us to concentrate on what we have been given and what we can give; to celebrate life; and to carry on his legacy of *pono* and *aloha*. ❧

Chapter Sixteen

TOWARD THE FUTURE

While many words like those in Randy Roth's eulogy were shared in the wake of King's passing, he had his own last word, in a way. In one of the final conversations with Jerry Burris and Ken Kobayashi leading to this book, King reminisced about his philosophy and his hopes and dreams for the future of his beloved Hawaiʻi.

I love Hawaiʻi, and in some ways I would like to think it will never change. But it will. It is changing rapidly already. We are going to become more and more like California. Why? Because California simply overwhelms us. They're something like the sixth-largest economy in the world. California people come over here, and they love it, and a lot of them stay here. They use what we have. And we already have resource problems, water in particular.

That concerns a lot of people, of course. But it matters particularly to the Hawaiians. I could feel that during the Kahoʻolawe trespassing trial with Walter Ritte and Emmett Aluli. They were sincere about their concern over the military bombing of Kahoʻolawe. It seemed to me the issue wasn't the military—although some people tried to make it that—but rather it was about Kahoʻolawe itself. The island isn't worth anything commercially, but that doesn't mean Kahoʻolawe is only good for bombing. Even if it never had much of a Hawaiian population, it remains sacred to some Hawaiians, and we should respect that. Around that time, the military was saying, "If we can't train on Kahoʻolawe, then we have to get out of here—leave the Islands." That was nonsense. They're not here for training; they're here because they are 3,000 miles closer to the Far East.

So while we in Hawaiʻi are a lot like the rest of the United States—and becoming more so—I think and hope that we will always be the Aloha State. Our only unique asset is that this is the home—and the only home—of the Hawaiian race and its culture. After 100 years of see-sawing policies, we are gradually coming to a more universal understanding that it is necessary to promote and preserve Hawaiian openness, the Hawaiian language, the Hawaiian approach to dispute resolution, the Hawaiian values of *aloha* and *pono*. I believe we have the best example in the world of reasonable peaceful existence among competing cultures and races, and that Hawaiians need to be leaders in preserving and improving this example of humanity at its best.

We live on islands—we can't get away from each other. If we want to stay in Hawai'i, we have to fix relations, not sever them. In Western law, we have an adversarial system, and all too often our legal system leaves little option other than to sue for damages if one is harmed by another. Somebody loses, somebody wins. Polynesians focus rather on reconciliation and consensus—what the Hawaiians call *ho'oponopono*, based on the Hawaiian concept of *pono*, doing something in the right way, the just way.

It's the same across Polynesia. In Samoa, there is a similar tradition of *ifoga*, in which one family renders a formal apology to another for a serious offense. Rather than punish the perpetrator, the goal is to bring peace and restore harmony between the families. The framers of the Constitution of the Federated States of Micronesia essentially adopted Western, or American, law as their basis, but they added that the constitution should be consistent with Micronesian customs and traditions. In other words, if there is no specific statute, courts are to substitute Micronesian customs and concepts of justice. This makes a lot of sense on a philosophical level. I wish we had more of that kind of latitude here in Hawai'i. After all, our state motto is *"Ua mau ke ea o ka 'aina i ka pono"*—the life of the land is preserved in *pono*, in righteousness.

In the long term, my hopeful view is that, as more and more Mainlanders move here, they will come here, fall in love with the place, and embrace the concept of *pono* and other qualities that help us get along on these tiny islands.

In my courtroom, I try to take into account what is *pono*, or right, as well as what the law says. This sounds like a Hawaiian thing, but it's really more universal. It's like that old saying that a good jurist is someone who knows how to temper justice with mercy. I even have hope for Californians. Earl Warren, the former governor of California, was a great chief justice. He always said he would determine what was fair and then come up with the legal basis accordingly. I agree with that philosophy.

As I get older, I think more and more about how the Earth has gone through all kinds of changes in history. What's now the North Pole was once the South Pole and the South Pole was once the North. Magnetic North has moved around.

My own North Star, the thing that keeps me focused and centered, is probably my wife, Anne, and my family, my parents.

The Earth today points toward the Polar Star, but it moves around. It wasn't always that way and it will change again, I'm sure. ❧

Appendix

A Law Clerk's Perspective

by Douglas Ushijima
Law Clerk 1992-93, 1994-95, 1998-2010

Judge King had fifty-six law clerks in his thirty-eight years as a federal judge. District judges are allocated two law clerks, who are attorneys that research the law, draft orders and opinions, and assist their judges with managing cases and other tasks. Sometimes called "elbow law clerks" because they work closely with a single judge, they may serve as sounding boards and advisors. Because of their role, most elbow law clerks gain unique perspectives on their judges, and with Judge King we saw him at his best.

Judge King began with a traditional model of hiring new graduates. He told one clerk that he liked to select law clerks from the law reviews of Ivy League schools "because they generally were liberal and could keep [me] honest." Later, he changed his mind. He didn't say if it was the "liberal" part or the "keep him honest" part that was wrong.

After a few years, he made it a point to hire at least one "local" clerk, someone from Hawai'i who could easily understand the context of cases. He taught by example and must have known his clerks would later contribute to Hawai'i. Many have gone on to serve as judges, government officials and prominent members of the bar—a type of legacy, so to speak. He believed in the University of Hawai'i Law School, hiring many of its graduates. He also hired women when others might not have; almost half his clerks were female.

Almost every King clerk loved their job and wanted to stay. But Judge King said his clerkships lasted a year because "after that, they start to think they're the judge." As he got older he switched to a newer model and hired a few clerks—who had learned never to "think they're the judge"—for longer periods.

"Puisne," Judge King he would call us. Puisne means "inferior in rank." It's pronounced *pyoo nee*, and his booming laugh would follow every time he said it. Every clerk remembers their first day answering the office phone when Judge King would call and ask, referring to himself, "Where is the lazy bum?" and then break out laughing as the clerk struggled to respond. It set the tone, and we soon came to know him as a wise and powerful man who knew his role, but didn't take himself too seriously.

Judge King wasn't overly concerned with material wealth. Federal judges must file an annual financial disclosure statement, available ostensibly so the public can check for conflicts of interest. Some judges don't like the intrusion, as others can measure their finances. Judge King, however, joked about the opposite effect: "I really don't like doing this; everyone can now see that I have nothing." But he did just fine, taking care of his family and choosing to travel whenever possible. He saw an expensive automobile at O'ahu Country Club and asked Mrs. King, "Do you want one of those, or shall we go to Paris for a month?" She answered, "Paris, of course."

At a clerk reunion, many clerks shared remembrances exemplifying his wit and wisdom. A clerk remembers him asking an assistant U.S. attorney to show an exhibit to the jury. When the prosecutor had difficulty finding it, Judge King quipped: "It's all right. I don't want to make a federal case out of this." Which says it all. Judge King was a federal judge who didn't want to make a federal case out of anything. He was an important man who didn't show it. An extraordinary man who embraced ordinary people. He didn't demand respect, but he always got it.

He used his quick wit to control the courtroom. Once, during a jury trial, the testimony of a defense witness was clearly aggravating the plaintiff ("Mr. Z."). Shortly after the witness finished testifying, Mr. Z took the stand and, red-faced and shaking with anger, thundered into the microphone, "Your Honor, may God strike me dead if that last witness wasn't lying!" Judge King, without missing a beat, replied, "Now there, Mr. Z, there's no reason to drag God into this. That's why we have a jury." This brought down the house (and calmed Mr. Z down).

Judge King often served on the Mainland. During a criminal hearing in California, counsel for the defendant complained to the judge about the government's tactics in bringing a conspiracy charge against his client. Judge King stated that it was no surprise to him how the government had acted, and without missing a beat, explained in a clear baritone voice that, in conspiracy cases, the government "throws its net out into the sea, and all the *humuhumunukunukuapua'a* come a-swimming to me." Makes perfect sense to someone from Hawai'i, but the Mainland counsel looked amusingly confused.

The Judge performed very heartwarming naturalization ceremonies in his courtroom. He instilled pride in each new citizen and urged every one of them to use wisely the precious gift they had just earned—the right to vote.

A lawyer told Judge King that he could not render a certain ruling because of a Ninth Circuit case. "If that is what the Ninth Circuit said, counselor," mused the judge, "then I'll give them another chance to say it."

Nevertheless, he followed the law, and later gave a corollary: "The Ninth Circuit affirmed me, and I still think I'm right." He adopted a practical philosophy. He said Judge Martin Pence told him early on, "they pay us to be decisive and do what we think is right; they pay the Ninth Circuit to fix our errors."

Judge King always defended Hawaiʻi's "cultural heritage." One clerk remembers a large antitrust case involving beer distributors, in which there was an argument over whether one of the plaintiffs was an appropriate class representative. Her name was something like Jade Flower Ogawa. One local attorney objected to her because she ran a "Korean bar." Mainland counsel objected to the objection, noting that Ms. Ogawa was not Korean, but was in fact Japanese. Judge King put the matter to rest by ruling that, "In Hawaiʻi, the term 'Korean bar' is a term of art."

It was not all fun and games. For a time, after Judge Dick Yin Wong died, Judge King was the only active judge and handled almost everything. He worked hard, often sitting by designation on the Ninth Circuit in his second favorite city, San Francisco. Judge King understood the power of his position and had an imposing presence. He knew the law and ran a tight courtroom with high expectations of lawyers who appeared before him.

His sense of humor came with a sense of human nature, of logic, of right and wrong. He was an "old-school," big-picture judge, not too caught up in the minutiae, with a perspective and wisdom few will ever have. He surrounded himself with his always-growing personal library and brought that and his vast life experiences to his judging. He inspired us all. ☙

A CHRONOLOGY:
THE LAW CLERKS OF JUDGE SAM KING

1.	Bruce Bigelow	1972-1973
2.	Kevin B. Hughes	1972-1973
3.	Charles H. Hurd	1972
4.	Charles L. Woltmann	1973-1974
5.	Archibald C.K. Kaolulo	1973-1974
6.	George Balis	1974
7.	William A. Cardwell II	1974-1975
8.	Anthony S. Chan	1975-1976
9.	Robert P. Feldman	1975-1976
10.	Susan Waggener	1976-1977
11.	Charles F. Gorder, Jr.	1976-1977
12.	Thomas K. Kaulukukui, Jr.	1977-1978
13.	Michiro Iwanaga	1977-1978
14.	Michael S. Cucchissi	1978-1979
15.	Louise Ing	1978-1979
16.	Deborah Ching	1979
17.	Philip Doi	1979
18.	Mark J. Bennett	1979-1980
19.	Karen L. Peterson	1979-1980
20.	Charlotte Schwab	1980-1981
21.	Allen K. Mukaida	1980-1981
22.	Steven G. Reade	1981-1982
23.	David W.K. Wong	1981-1982
24.	Laird M. Robertson	1982-1983
25.	Kathryn S. Matayoshi	1982-1983
26.	Mark J. Coleman	1983-1984
27.	Sharyl Walker	1983-1984

28.	Richard G. Wallace	1984-1985
29.	Lyn Anzai	1984-1985
30.	C. Brandon Wisoff	1985-1986
31.	Leslie Allen	1985-1986
32.	Joyce E. McCarty	1986-1987
33.	K. James Steiner, Jr.	1986-1987
34.	Hannah Rabkin	1987-1988
35.	Brad S. Petrus	1987-1988
36.	Laurie Kuribayashi	1988-1989
37.	Michael J. Morris	1988-1989
38.	Lisa M. Ginoza	1989-1990
39.	Robert Lee Wilkerson	1989-1990
40.	Dawn R. Ross	1990-1991
41.	Gaye Y. Tatsuno	1990-1991
42.	David F. Andrew	1991-1992
43.	Trisha M. Kimura	1991-1992
44.	Douglas Ushijima	1992-1993
45.	Ann-Marie McKittrick	1992-1993
46.	Geoffrey K.S. Komeya	1993-1994
47.	Donna H. Kalama	1993-1994
(44)	Douglas Ushijima	1994-1995
48.	David Harada-Stone	1994-1995
49.	Emily Kawashima Waters	1995-1996
50.	Colleen E. Boyle	1995-1996
51.	Robert W. Wachter	1996-1997
52.	Carol A. Uyeno	1996-1997
(49)	Emily Kawashima Waters	1997-1998
53.	Stacey Kawasaki Djou	1997-1998
54.	Sandra Wilhide	1998-1999
55.	Elijah Yip	1999-2001
56.	Tatyana Cerullo	2001
(49)	Emily Kawashima Waters	2002-2004
(44)	Douglas Ushijima	1998-2001

Appendix

Hawaiʻi—An Integral Part of the United States

National Oratorical Contest Finals Speech,
Washington, D.C., May 1933

I come to you tonight from a land five thousand miles away. It is a group of islands in the mid-Pacific, swept by the fresh tradewinds, green and lovely under the tropic sun, sparkling in a sea of azure and emerald. Once peopled only by brown Polynesians whose blood flows in my own veins, it is a now a territory of the United States. It is a strategic point in the great Pacific area, and harmonious melting pot of many races, and as a part of our common country it relies upon the principles of the Constitution for a full measure of justice. It is on that constitution and its immediate, its vital bearing on Hawaiʻi today, that I speak to you.

Hawaiʻi is one of only two territories to be incorporated into the United States from the status of a sovereign nation. She was acquired neither by purchase, conquest, nor discovery, but was annexed of her own volition by joint resolution of Congress in 1898. A treaty of annexation was pending at that time, but it did not go through. So Hawaiʻi became a part of the national domain, subject to the general clause of the Constitution which gives Congress full power over the territory or other property of the United States. By that provision the federal legislature could have abolished all Hawaiian laws and completely reorganized Hawaiʻi's government. However, Congress not only allowed the government of the former Republic of Hawaiʻi to continue in operation for nearly two years after annexation, but also, by the Organic Act of 1900, finally established Hawaiʻi as an incorporated territory on exactly the same basis as the other territories of the United States, all of which have become states except Alaska. Also, upon the recommendation of a Congressional committee, which visited the islands and made a thorough survey of conditions, American citizenship was extended to all the citizens of Hawaiʻi, regardless of race, under the same laws as apply here on the Mainland. The Supreme Court of the United States further defined Hawaiʻi's status by deciding in the famous "insular cases" that the Constitution did follow the flag to Hawaiʻi in full force and effect, which is not true in regard to Puerto Rico or the Philippines.

It is not surprising that Hawai'i should have been endorsed so completely, for during the better part of a century before annexation she had been under the influence of the great American commonwealth. Soon after the arrival of the missionaries in 1820 Christianity became the religion of the country, and the American principle of religious toleration was accepted as fundamental. Universal education was early established, and before annexation a free, compulsory educational system in the English language was in force. In the evolution of Hawai'i's government American models were followed, so that when the Organic Act went into effect, practically the whole body of Hawaiian law remained in force because there was nothing in it inconsistent with the Constitution. Hawai'i's trade was from earliest days largely with America, and after 1876, when a reciprocity treaty was negotiated between the two nations, the Hawaiian Islands became very closely linked with the United States. So in her interests and in the body of her culture, Hawai'i was an American community before she became an actual part of the American nation.

Since annexation Hawai'i has taken her responsibilities seriously and has entered into American life with energy. She has carried her share and more of the same burdens as every other part of the United States. The constitution and its amendments automatically apply to Hawai'i, and nearly all the general laws of Congress, especially the fiscal and restrictive legislation, include the islands. Hawai'i has a credit balance in the federal treasury from federal taxes of some $140,000,000. Hawai'i's people, no matter of what race, look to America for their higher education, in many cases for their life's work, and in all cases for their allegiance. At the time of the World War Hawai'i contributed her quota to the nation's effort. Spiritually, economically, and politically, Hawai'i has shown herself to be American.

What I have been saying, we of Hawai'i recognize and accept without question. But there has been an intimation recently that people here on the Mainland do not understand or appreciate these facts. In brief, there have been bills introduced in Congress to lessen the degree of Hawai'i's self-government as now enjoyed. Although under the Constitution this action is legally possible, there is in the circumstances of Hawai'i's annexation and in her history, a moral obligation on the part of the United States to continue her as an organized territory with every right to aspire to ultimate statehood. In full confidence that America recognized this obligation, and in the conviction that her destiny was determined by the territorial precedents of American history, Hawai'i placed her fate in the hands of the American nation without reservation. Let not the American people betray that trust. ❧

Appendix

JUSTICE AND EQUALITY
DEPEND UPON LAW—AND YOU!

Law Day USA Speech,
Pearl Harbor Commissioned Officers' Mess, May 1969

We should be listening to a dropout from society who has different thoughts, experiences and values, who challenges the established order. What would such a speaker say about our theme? In the absence of the real thing, I will attempt to play the role of this turned-off speaker and myself in succession, and see what happens.

At the outset, my alter ego suggests that justice and equality are not largely irrelevant, that the modern goals should be love and freedom. If we love one another, justice becomes a byproduct of our humanity. Where there is unrestricted freedom, there is universal equality.

But this comparison is not quite fair. Justice and equality may not be the only desirable objectives of an organized society, but they are important objectives. Life teaches us to beware of oversimplification. The battle for the good must be fought on many fronts at the same time. If we try to love our neighbor but he will not love us, we must have secondary positions to occupy. Unrestricted freedom raises the eternal problem of what to do about the bad guys. Try again.

You say justice and equality are desirable objectives. What is justice? When the convicted defendant pleaded for mercy, the judge retorted: "Mercy! You do not get mercy in a court of law. You get justice." Again, I remind you of the dictum: "The best way to get rid of a bad law is to enforce it." Yet if you keep changing the rules to fit each particular situation, you have abandoned the traditional tests of a just result and substituted "fundamental fairness," which is simply humanity.

Equality has always allowed for unequal treatment. Convicted felons, the mentally un-normal, married women, children, American Indians, immigrants and, more recently, the poor and the black, among others, have been subjects of special rules not applicable to everybody else. In each case, the classification is sought to be justified as reasonable and often as beneficial, too, and equality is asserted within the class—but the net result is still inequality.

George Orwell gave us the definitive explanation: "All people are created equal, but some are created more equal than others." Anatole France gave us the definitive criticism when he alluded to "the majestic equality of the law, which forbids the rich as well as the poor to sleep under bridges, to beg in the streets, and to steal bread."

Well, these are bitter characterizations of noble principles. We do not claim perfection. We do insist on a striving toward perfection. Our theme acknowledges that bad law and bad people can produce less than acceptable justice or equality. Admitting that good intentions are not enough, yet separation of persons into classes is justified by other sublime principles. The point is not so much that classifications are made, but that when the conditions change the classifications should be reexamined and modified appropriately.

The challenge is immediate. Inequalities, my other charge says, create power advantages and those who are advantaged release their power as a result of sweet reason. Only confrontation and violent action can shift the power distribution. If you counter that in a democracy this can be accomplished peacefully at the ballot box, the refutation is that those who are more unequal today are disenfranchised either legally, as in the case of minors, or illegally, as in the case of black people.

This could be a valid criticism of our society if nothing were being done to correct the situation, or if what is being done is too little and too late. I think we in the establishment are meeting our responsibilities. You think we are not. The ultimate answer is in the actual results. When events are taking place, the participants are usually the least able to judge objectively. Time will tell. But at least we are trying.

There is more to the antiestablishment position than comparative rectitude, says our second guest. You are talking about patching up the system here and there. I am talking about an entirely new structure to our institutions. Biennial popular elections, representative government, regional sovereignty, written constitutions, bureaucracies—these structures are too unwieldy and unresponsive to meet the needs of the atomic age. We are fighting a war that almost nobody wants to continue, we are polluting the air and the sea, we are overpopulating the Earth, we are becoming slaves of the automobile and yet we are unable to take decisive action to solve any of these problems. More than that, the problems themselves arose out of a reward-oriented work culture that emphasizes competition for material wealth. Other styles of living give one a more satisfying life. Laws passed by traditional legislatures are not going to improve the situation. Almost 200 years of legislating in the U.S.A. have produced volumes and volumes of law, yet our problems now are more serious than when we had fewer laws.

What is required is a new society based on new values and governed by new methods. The details have not settled out, but the change is coming. Hopefully it will come in time to save us from self-destruction.

Well, now. "Law" as used in our theme means, no doubt, the rule of law as opposed to rule by individual fiat. Surely we must also infer that good laws are implied and that regulatory codes, written or customary, enforced by sub-governments such as corporations, labor unions, fraternal organizations and the like, are included. Without these qualifications, we would have to construct a model that embraces Nazi Germany, which was legalistic but unjust, and this would be impermissible.

With regard to the other points, we, too, are concerned. Change is easier in the U.S.A. than in most other parts of the world but solutions are harder. Everybody is an expert, especially everybody under thirty. I wish I could be as sure of anything as our friends under thirty are of everything. Still, I like miniskirts and Nehru jackets, I think universities should be citadels of learning and not commercial plants engaged in the business of research, I agree that the level of teaching would improve if students evaluated the teachers, and I quit cigarette smoking five years ago. On the other hand I am not convinced that blowing pot will materially assist in meeting reality, or that terrorizing professors will improve higher education, or that use of obscenity clarifies communication.

The French have an apt aphorism: "Plus ça change, plus c'est la même chose." It is not difficult to prove that a benevolent dictatorship is the best form of government or that hedonism is the most attractive philosophy of life. But no one has yet solved the problem of keeping a dictatorship benevolent or the problem of supporting a life of pleasure. Power does tend to corrupt, and absolute power does corrupt absolutely; and even hedonists need to have somebody engage in unpleasurable activities to produce the wherewithal for the hedonists to practice hedonism. It is both a blessing and a curse that each generation of man is born ignorant. Unfortunately, the process of aging does not guarantee that this condition is corrected in adults. A little mutual respect will go a long way toward bridging the apparent chasm in understanding.

Finally my rebellious friend pronounces the clincher. That word YOU in your theme doesn't include me. I am the victim of injustice and equality. There is nothing for me to do to promote justice and equality. You others are the perpetrators of the wrongs inflicted on me. YOU means the ones with power, the advantaged, the members of the establishment.

Here I am on firmer ground when I assert positively that my other me is in error. YOU means everybody—every man, woman and child. Our system of criminal justice depends very largely upon the acquiescence and even support of those charged with crime. If any substantial number of persons refuses to assent to the provisions of a criminal law, it might as well be repealed as to them. In this category are the crimes of adultery, fornication and sodomy.

A spectacular example of the rule of law in operation was furnished by the Washington, D.C., municipal courts at the time of the rioting there in 1967. Hundreds of persons were rounded up by the Army and delivered to the courthouse. The result was chaos. Those defendants could have taken over the entire building, ejected all the officials and never been identified. Yet they submitted to the processing with only minor rebellion. The courts had many serious problems, but assent to the laws to be enforced was not one of them.

The history of Prohibition furnishes the opposite lesson. So many persons refused to assent to the Prohibition amendment and subsequent legislation that these laws were never effectively enforced and finally had to be modified.

Surveying the path we have been traveling, we find a good deal of wreckage and some litter along the way, but our theme has survived the ordeal.

"Justice and Equality Depend upon Law—and YOU!" ᕽ

Appendix

CHURCH AND STATE

Speech at Temple Emmanuel, Honolulu, December 1984

Rabbi Magid invited me to speak to you tonight on "Church and State" issues in the light of recent decisions of the Supreme Court. I am happy to do so, as much for my own edification as for any contribution I may be able to make to your thinking in this area.

Being a judge, and having once been a lawyer, I tend to take a legalistic approach. Yet there are other considerations besides legality. I do not wish to leave you with the impression that, because an action is legal, or more precisely not illegal, it is therefore unobjectionable. It is not illegal to commit suicide, but most moral codes condemn that act.

I am constrained also, in the interest of time and clarity, to limit myself to one subject that I believe would be currently of most interest to you, and that is the Establishment Clause of the First Amendment to our federal Constitution. I propose to discuss two recent Supreme Court decisions applying this clause and to analyze what these decisions portend for the future. In this connection, I will look backward at the historical context in which the original amendment was adopted and forward at what has happened since those decisions.

For those of you who do not speak legalese, let me define the Establishment Clause. That part of the First Amendment that relates specifically to religion provides: "Congress shall make no law respecting an establishment of religion, or prohibiting the free exercise thereof." The first part of that provision is referred to as the Establishment Clause and the second part is referred to as the Free Exercise Clause. Generally speaking, the Free Exercise Clause relates to religious activities by individuals, and the Establishment Clause relates to religious activities by government.

An example of a Free Exercise application is the 1964 case of *People v. Woody*, in which the California Supreme Court held that the members of the Native American Church had a constitutional right to use peyote in religious services. In case you did not know it, peyote contains a psychedelic drug and is proscribed by both federal and state criminal laws.

An example of an Establishment Clause application is the 1979 case of *Malnak v. Yogi* in which the federal Third Circuit Court of Appeals enjoined the New Jersey public schools from presenting an optional course in Creative Intelligence-Transcendental Meditation in which students heard teachers chant and make offerings to a deified "guru Dev."

Narrowing our inquiry to matters concerning the Establishment Clause, we note firstly that the First Amendment prohibitions refer only to laws passed by Congress. Indeed, until the adoption of the Fourteenth Amendment in 1868, it was clear that these prohibitions did not apply to the several states. Eventually the Supreme Court developed the doctrine that the Due Process Clause of the Fourteenth Amendment incorporated certain rights and protections set forth in the Bill of Rights. In 1940, the Free Exercise Clause was so applied to the States. In 1947, the Establishment Clause was so applied to the States. Thus, for at least the first 160 years of our Union, the States were free from any federal constitutional restraints in matters of religion.

Does this mean that a state was free to have an established religion? Yes. In fact, most of the original thirteen states did have established state religions. The 1778 Constitution of South Carolina, for example, decreed, "the Christian Protestant religion shall be deemed, and is hereby constituted and declared to be the established religion of this State." New Jersey's 1776 Constitution 3, which remained in force until 1844, restricted public office to believers in Protestantism. So also was Protestantism preferred in New Hampshire, Pennsylvania, Delaware, Maryland and Virginia. Under Maryland's Declaration of Rights of 1776, only persons "professing the Christian religion" were entitled to religious freedom, and it was not until 1826 that Jews were permitted to hold public office in that state.

Of course, this early discrimination gradually ended, at least insofar as it was supported by law. New states were admitted with constitutions containing bills of rights similar to the federal Constitution. Older states amended their constitutions to conform. And once the Supreme Court had incorporated the First Amendment into the Fourteenth Amendment, all states became subject to the same minimum prohibitions enunciated by the Supreme Court.

As an aside, I wish to emphasize the word "minimum." There is a growing body of law to the effect that states are free to interpret their own constitutions as providing more extensive protections within a state than the federal Constitution even when the provision being applied is word for word the same in the state constitution as in the federal Constitution. This is a subject for another time, but the principle should be kept in mind.

Returning to the early history of religious bigotry in the several states, one may well ask how the First Amendment became part of our Constitution. For one thing, those states practicing religious discrimination differed as to who were the discriminators and who were the discriminatees. Thus, each state had a stake in preventing the other states from imposing an alien form of discrimination.

Then, too, in each state there was a fear of being subjected to the kinds of oppression imposed by a central government in support of an established church. An "establishment" of religion suggested several characteristics. These were:

- A state church officially recognized and protected by the sovereign.
- A state church whose members alone were eligible to vote, to hold public office and to practice a profession.
- A state church which compelled religious orthodoxy under penalty of fine and imprisonment.
- A state church willing to expel dissenters from the commonwealth.
- A state church financed by taxes upon all members of the community.
- A state church which alone could freely hold public worship and evangelize.
- A state church which alone could perform valid marriages, burials and other ceremonial acts.

If these were important concerns in the phrasing of the Establishment Clause of the First Amendment, what has the Supreme Court done to give legal definition to the word "establishment?" As I said earlier, nothing much in the way of litigation reached the Supreme Court until the 1940s. Over the years, the Court has declared that the Establishment Clause was violated whenever there was excessive government entanglement with religious institutions and whenever there was government endorsement or disapproval of religion. In 1971, in the case of *Lemon v. Kurtzman*, the court articulated a three-part test as a guide to detecting unconstitutional government action. To pass an Establishment Clause challenge:

- First, the government action must have a secular purpose.
- Second, the principal or primary effect of the action must be one that neither advances nor inhibits religion.
- Third, the action must not foster an excessive government entanglement with religion.

Has this three-part test solved Establishment Clause Controversies? No. It has not.

My father used to quote an earlier realist with the statement: "Grant you your general proposition if you'll grant me each particular instance."

The pitfalls in this area may be illustrated by following the opinions of two great Supreme Court justices, Justice Douglas and Justice Brennan. In 1952, Justice Douglas wrote:

"We are a religious people whose institutions presuppose a Supreme Being. We guarantee the freedom to worship as one chooses. We make room for as wide a variety of beliefs and creeds as the spiritual needs of man deem necessary. We sponsor an attitude on the part of government that shows no partiality to any one group and that lets each flourish according to the zeal of its adherents and the appeal of its dogma. When the state encourages religious instruction or cooperates with religious authorities by adjusting the schedule of public events to sectarian needs, it follows the best of our traditions. For it then respects the religious nature of our people and accommodates the public service to their spiritual needs. To hold that it may not would be to find in the Constitution a requirement that the government show a callous indifference to religious groups. That would be preferring those who believe in no religion over those who do believe. Government may not finance religious groups nor undertake religious instruction nor blend secular and sectarian education nor use secular institutions to force one or some religion on any person. But we find no constitutional requirement which makes it necessary for government to be hostile to religion and to throw its weight against efforts to widen the effective scope of religious influence . . ."

In later years, Justice Douglas became the Court's most extreme separationist.

Justice Brennan went through a similar metamorphosis. In a concurring opinion in 1963 he wrote:

"The saying of invocational prayers in legislative chambers, state or federal, and the appointment of legislative chaplains, might well represent no involvements of the kind prohibited by the Establishment Clause. Legislators, federal and state, are mature adults who may presumably absent themselves from such public and ceremonial exercises without incurring any penalty, direct or indirect."

When that precise issue finally came before the Court in 1983, Justice Brennan had changed his mind. "I now believe," he said, "that the practice of official invocational prayer, as it exists in . . . most . . . State Legislatures, is unconstitutional."

All of the foregoing is prologue to two recent Supreme Court pronouncements, one in *Marsh v. Chambers* in 1983, and one in *Lynch v. Donnelly* in 1984.

In Marsh the Court held that the Nebraska Legislature had not violated the Establishment Clause by employing a salaried chaplain to pray at the beginning of each session. The chaplain in question was of the Presbyterian faith, had been continuously so employed for sixteen years, and gave prayers in the Judeo-Christian tradition. For example, his opening two sentences on March 20, 1978, were:

"Father in heaven, the suffering and death of your son brought life to the world moving our hearts to praise your glory. The power of the cross reveals your concern for the world and the wonder of Christ crucified."

The Court split 6 to 3—Chief Justice Burger writing for himself and Justices White, Blackmun, Powell, Rehnquist and O'Connor. Justices Brennan, Marshall and Stevens dissented. The Chief Justice relied on historical patterns and practices to conclude that "the practice of opening sessions with prayer has become part of the fabric of our society." He declared the practice to be "a tolerable acknowledgment of beliefs widely held among the people of this country."

Justice Brennan pointed out that the chief justice had not even attempted to apply the *Lemon v. Kurtzman* three-part test. Justice Stevens thought that having the same chaplain for sixteen years giving "clearly sectarian" prayers was going beyond any permissible government religious activity.

In *Lynch v. Donnelly* the Court held that the city of Pawtucket, Rhode Island, had not violated the Establishment Clause by supporting with public funds the erection and maintenance of a crèche as part of a Christmas display which included a Santa Claus house, a Christmas tree and a banner reading "Seasons Greetings," in a private park in the heart of the city's shopping district.

The Court split 5 to 4, the chief justice writing for the majority. This time Justice Blackmun joined Justices Brennan, Marshall and Stevens in dissent. Justice O'Connor wrote a separate concurring opinion.

The chief justice thought that when "viewed in the proper context of the Christmas Holiday season, it is apparent that, on this record, there is insufficient evidence to establish that the inclusion of the crèche is a purposeful or surreptitious effort to express some kind of subtle governmental advocacy of a particular religious message." He declared that there were legitimate secular purposes for the display and that the primary effect was not to advance religion. His analysis was based on the *Lemon v. Kurtzman* test, as was everybody else's, but with differing results.

It should be noted that, in both cases, the lower federal courts—district courts and circuit courts of appeal—had ruled unanimously that the practices in question did violate the Establishment Clause.

Usually after a Supreme Court decision on a controversial issue there is much speculation on where we go from here. The chief justice in Marsh quoted Justice Holmes to the effect that those who felt threatened need have no fear "while this Court sits." I did not find that same quote in *Lynch v. Donnelly*. Yet it is true that one case does not necessarily decide the ultimate boundaries of a doctrine. To the extent that minority groups feel that their rights are still threatened, and majority groups feel that their rights are still ignored, the Marsh and Donnelly cases have raised more questions than they have answered.

Crèches have been taken out of storage in several towns throughout the country. The ACLU has been busy filing suits to enjoin the activity. Where only the crèche has been displayed, the lower courts have enjoined government subsidy. A federal district judge in Birmingham, Michigan, ruled that displaying a crèche alone could not be considered nonsectarian. The Dearborn City Council sold its city-owned nativity scene and a small plot of land where it was located to a private foundation to circumvent a federal judge's order that the scene be removed. In Chicago, the city removed a crèche display after receiving complaints but without court action.

It is likely that the tradition of government-funded religious displays will come to an end and be an activity only of private citizens, as proposed by Michigan's ACLU director.

The next issue will be whether private citizens have a right to use public land for a religious display. A case involving that question is, in fact, now before the Supreme Court. The Supreme Court's recent pronouncements under the Establishment Clause can be, and I am confident will be narrowly applied. The ultimate result will probably be a strengthening of private religious activity. The ongoing debate is healthy and will help hold the line against creeping establishmentism.

The price of liberty is still eternal vigilance. ❧

Appendix

Keynote Address

Japan-Hawaiʻi Lawyers' Association, Hiroshima, Japan, April, 1985

We are indebted to many persons for this historic gathering. My involvement with the Japan-Hawaiʻi Lawyers' Association has been only in Honolulu up to this time. So I am most acquainted with the effort put in by our President Mark Shklov, with the able assistance of Vice President Audrey Kitagawa, Treasurer Calvert Chipchase, Secretary Blake Okimoto and member Richard Kantor. When I first heard of the possibility of this convention at Hiroshima, it was just a dream of Mark's. That it has become a reality is a testament to what can be accomplished by persistence, hard work and dedication to an idea.

As Mark's plans progressed, he was fortunate to have the enthusiastic support of the University of Hawaiʻi's Richardson School of Law in the persons of then Dean Richard Miller and his successor Acting Dean Jeremy Harrison, and especially of Professor John Vafai. Professor Vafai secured grant funds from an agency of the United States with which to bring to this convention learned members of the faculty of the law school and to pay some of the expenses of the convention. Through Professor Vafai we have been able to bring a high level of professionalism to this meeting. Of course the work done at this end of the joint endeavor was crucial. The original idea might well have come from Tokyo member Robert McIlroy. He and members Professor Hiroyuki Hata of Hiroshima University, attorney Ryokuji Shiinoki of this city and Kazuya Maruyama of Tokyo have been the contacts and workhorses for the myriad details that had to be handled in Japan.

The Japan-Hawaiʻi Lawyers' Association, Inc., is a nonprofit Hawaiʻi corporation, which was formed on June 26, 1981, by the officers mentioned earlier. There are some seventy members, about ten of whom are in Japan. I have to make particular mention of U.S. Consul Lawrence Enomoto, stationed in Okinawa, because he was at one time a student in my class on federal courts at the law school in Hawaiʻi.

We are most honored by the presence of the Governor of Hiroshima Prefecture, His Excellency Toranosuke Takeshita, and of the Mayor of

Hiroshima, the Honorable Takeshi Araki. This morning at the opening ceremonies you heard a message of goodwill and good wishes from the Governor of Hawai'i, His Excellency George Ariyoshi. I have here also a message from the Mayor of the City and County of Honolulu, the Honorable Frank F. Fasi.

On a personal note, I feel a special relationship to this city. I was in Honolulu on December 7, 1941, and I toured Hiroshima by Jeep on September 15, 1945. Between those two events, I had become a Japanese-language interpreter for the United States Navy, in the course of which I met my wife, who was in the same program. I came back to Japan for several years thereafter on annual training duty with the Navy, but never back to Hiroshima.

I also became addicted to the game of Go. I had been exposed to the game at the U.S. Navy Language School at Boulder, Colorado, where Japanese citizens stranded in the United States taught us much about the culture of Japan. In 1965, Dr. George Leckie and I were the co-translators and co-editors of *The Theory and Practice of Go* by O. Korschelt, which is printed in Japan by Charles Tuttle.

That is why I took note of the fact that on August 6, 1945, the second game of the third series of the Honinbo Title tournament between Hashimoto and Iwamoto was being played in the outskirts of Hiroshima. The game was supposed to have been played in Dr. Fujii's house near the center of the city, but the city police insisted that the game be cancelled or moved elsewhere. It had taken Hashimoto twenty hours to come to Hiroshima from Osaka. He was delayed by air raids and had to spend a night at Mihara. The game had begun on August 4 and was to be concluded on August 6. The nuclear explosion reached out to the outskirts and shook the house where the game was being played. Glass windowpanes crashed in a thousand pieces. One hundred and six Black and White stones scattered everywhere in the room.

Thinking that the explosion was just from an ordinary bomb, the contestants resumed the game after sweeping the glass pieces off the mats. The game concluded that afternoon. Hashimoto as White won by five points. Naturally, when the participants found out what had happened, they were most chagrined at having taken it all so calmly.

That August 1945 explosion over this city was a terrible event in the history of mankind, and one which mankind must prevent from ever happening again. The attainment of world peace is the most important duty of our leaders, yet we all have a responsibility to exert our best efforts to the same end. Lest we lose our sense of urgency in this struggle, Hiroshima exists as a reminder that our goal has not been achieved until the chance of nuclear war has been rendered impossible.

We lawyers and judges and law professors may not be able to guarantee peace in our world, but we can and do make substantial contributions to peace. After all, our training centers around dispute resolution. It is our function in society to identify the points of conflict between individuals, develop the facts, apply accepted principles and reach just conclusions.

Within a single country, our activities may well be limited to disputes and conflicts that relate to internal harmony. What we do at home in handling divorce cases, breach of contract suits, civil rights actions, etcetera has little bearing on world peace. But when we cross over our national boundaries and concern ourselves with disputes and conflicts that arise between persons in different countries, we build bonds of understanding and friendship that ease the way to dispute resolution in international transactions.

I do not mean to claim too much for this modest beginning. We are not here to fashion solutions to disputes between nations. I do maintain that in relations between peoples of different countries, every increase in understanding, and every expansion of friendship, and every consensus on a procedure for resolving disputes, makes international harmony—and therefore world peace—more likely.

Today we have discussed doing business in Japan, nuclear waste, collective bargaining and divorce. Tomorrow we discuss intellectual property rights in this age of high technology, alternative dispute resolution, immigration requirements, energy policy, real estate law and real estate investment, and personal injury law. That is a wide range of topics, dictated in part by the talent available among our members and from the participating law schools. All of the discussions have, however, the same focus—a comparison of Japanese and American approaches to similar problems in business or personal relationships.

We start with the assumption that the legal systems of two dissimilar countries are also dissimilar. In general, this is usually true. Yet we often discover that the practical results of dissimilar systems are substantially the same. Whether one is trained in an adversary system, or an accusatory system, or an inquisitorial system, or a parental system, the human problems and the desired resolutions are essentially the same. We do not look for uniformity, but rather we seek to learn from each other new or better principles or procedures to apply to these human problems to reach these desired resolutions.

The latest trend in jurisprudence in the United States is "alternative dispute resolution." In Seattle a form of mediation is conducted under a court rule. In San Francisco, New Haven and Philadelphia, forms of mandatory arbitration under court rule are being tried as demonstration projects. In Cleveland, Judge Thomas D. Lambros has devised what he calls a summary jury trial. In Honolulu, we have the Neighborhood Justice Center, which tries to mediate neighborhood disputes without court involvement.

Another fruitful source of alternative methods of dispute resolution is comparative law—the study of how some other country handles the same or similar disputes. To a large extent, that is what we are doing here.

It is, of course, interesting to listen to descriptions of each other's legal systems. It is, however, more important to take away from this convention ideas and concepts out of one system that might be useful in the other system.

These, then, are our plans and hopes for this first Japan-Hawai'i Lawyers' Association Convention:

- One, that it may become an annual or biannual meeting into the foreseeable future
- Two, that it may lead to professional contacts and friendships that will endure
- Three, that it may develop a better understanding between the legal communities represented here
- Four, that it may produce research and literature on legal issues of mutual interest
- Five, that all of us who have participated will leave with a feeling of having been enriched spiritually, emotionally, and intellectually

I am confident that the same spirit of cooperation and professionalism, the same feeling of mutual respect and friendship, the same willingness to work and persevere, in the successful holding of this convention, will continue hereafter in the attainment of all of these goals.

I thank you for your kind attention. ❧

Appendix

THE NEW HAWAIIAN IDENTITY

Chaminade University Commencement Speech, Honolulu, December 1986

Mr. Chairman, Father Roesch, honored guests, fellow students, family and well-wishers, ladies and gentlemen: Aloha. I am honored to have been invited to participate in these commencement exercises. The 50th anniversary of my own graduation from college is just a few months away, and I remember that occasion as one that was viewed with joy, relief and pride. I sense that you greet this ceremony with similar feelings. You are also aware, I am sure, that you are soon to be privileged to join the ranks of alumni and alumnae who will receive annual requests for financial contributions to your most deserving alma mater.

My remarks will be directed more specifically to you graduating students. This is your night and we are all here because of you. Also, as you will discover in the course of my remarks, I am asking you to be role models in the future of human relationships in Hawai'i.

In one sense I bring you good news and bad news—good news in that Hawai'i will be a better place for all of us, bad news in that you will have to work at bringing about the good news.

My subject tonight is the future of the relationships among the several groups that make Hawai'i their home. Among you there are representatives of most of the diverse races, racial mixtures and cultural backgrounds in Hawai'i. You are together an example of Hawai'i's best. Furthermore, with your education, you are necessarily leaders in directing the forces now at work among us. How we get along with each other will depend in large part upon the examples set by you and others like you who are young, educated and raring to go.

Interracial harmony in Hawai'i has evolved past its earlier dependence on the all-embracing quality of the Hawaiian spirit of aloha to its present reliance on mutual respect among separate minority groups. The next development will be a newer approach to co-existence that draws from the best features of past and present to lead toward a new Hawaiian identity.

To the world in the 1930s, Hawai'i was a model of interracial relationships. We were "the melting pot of the Pacific." We credited the Hawaiian concepts of aloha, *'ohana*, *kokua* and *ho'oponopono* with much of the success achieved in the integration of our different racial groups. *Aloha* in the sense of caring about others and in which we can recognize elements of Christian love. *'Ohana* in the sense of community collaboration for mutual benefit among those living in close proximity with one another and in which we can recognize elements of the clan but without any required blood relationship. *Ho'oponopono* as a problem-solving technique in which we can recognize elements of participatory democracy. *Kokua* as the basis for an economic system based on cooperation and in which we can recognize elements of the business cooperative. Interracial marriage was accepted as a desirable happening by most observers but was not a necessary condition for mutual interaction.

The 1980s present a different picture. Interracial marriage has accelerated, but the anticipated homogeneity has not come about. We are a community in which minority status is pursued. The current fad is to emphasize and extol our differences, which are then made the basis for special demands expressed in strident voice and militant language. This follows in part from a laudable effort to preserve cultural heritages. But it has been encouraged also by ill-considered governmental actions and subsidies that make a virtue of divergence.

Perhaps the melting pot ideal was unrealistic. Certainly the multiplication of minority groupings is self-defeating. There is good news, however, in the newer approach to co-existence that is emerging and which will be the future basis for our interrelationships. Forces now at work portend that the future will bring significant changes in racial and cultural emphasis. Let me deal briefly with what I see as the most important of these changes.

1. *"Hawaiian" culture and values will be more pervasive.*
I believe that there is a growing realization that our most special possession is our Hawaiian inheritance. The voters of Hawai'i recognized the concerns of Hawaiians, and the value to all residents of Hawai'i of addressing these concerns, by adopting the constitutional provisions relating to the Office of Hawaiian Affairs. OHA is gradually getting its act together, is becoming a positive force in right directions, and deserves our enthusiastic support.

Hawaiian music, dance and sports have spread around the world. All three activities need, and will receive, more financial support. Hawaiian music is at least as appealing as country music—to me anyway. The hula is more accessible to everyone than, say, the ballet. Hawaiians invented surfing. We should be doing more to promote our leadership in all three areas. There is much more going on in academia and elsewhere in preserving Hawaiian values.

2. Points of conflict and antagonism will be eliminated or softened.

The distribution and use of land, and the distribution and exercise of political power, have been continuing sources of friction in our society. The limitation of the executive term to eight years and the reapportionment of the Legislature to single districts have removed most legitimate cause for complaint in the political area. It remains, perhaps, to provide more local government by permitting the organization of self-governing townships such as Waipahu, Wai'anae, Kāne'ohe, Kailua-Kona and others.

Land distribution is still a thorny issue that resists easy solutions. However, the application of Hawai'i's pioneering leasehold condemnation law has done much to ameliorate homeowner dissatisfaction with tenant status. Since the law applies without question to leaseholds entered into after its passage, this source of conflict will disappear.

3. The rhetoric of disagreement will be softer, less defensive and less divisive.

When Queen Lili'uokalani was overthrown, there were less than 90,000 persons in the entire kingdom, of whom less than 35,000 were Hawaiians and another 6,200 were part-Hawaiians. By 1960, under the same definitions (the definitions changed after 1960), of a total population of 633,000, there were 11,300 Hawaiians and 91,000 part-Hawaiians. The part-Hawaiians include, along with their Hawaiian blood, every other racial extraction in Hawai'i. Thus it is clear that, in the long run, the Hawaiian cause cannot be successful by attempting to alienate every other racial group. The intelligent and reasoned promotion of specific proposals will succeed, as it has with the creation of OHA. This approach leaves room for aggressiveness if not for belligerence.

4. There will be a renewed pride in being "Hawaiian."

I was shocked a few years ago to hear a leading part-Hawaiian say publicly that he had been brought up to be ashamed of his Hawaiian blood. I was brought up to be proud of my Hawaiian blood, and I always have been. It never occurred to me that anyone would be less than proud of having Hawaiian ancestors.

I am reminded of the story of the two psychiatrists who had offices in the same building—one on the fourth floor and one on the tenth floor. Whenever they were on the same elevator, the fourth-floor psychiatrist, before exiting, would spit in the face of the tenth-floor psychiatrist, who did nothing about it except to wipe his face clean. Another tenant of the building who had observed this event on several occasions could not contain his curiosity. "Why does that fellow spit in your face?" he asked the tenth-floor psychiatrist. The tenth-floor psychiatrist answered, "That's his problem."

So, if anyone is ashamed of being Hawaiian or part-Hawaiian, that really is his personal problem. Far from being undesirables, the Hawaiians were too much in demand as wives and husbands, which accounts for so many part-Hawaiians compared to full-blood Hawaiians.

These predictions are all based on my interpretation of current activities by many groups and individuals. I believe that they are valid conclusions from observable facts. I am also firmly of the opinion that the resulting cultural and racial mix will make ours an even more fascinating and stimulating society. I ask you to bend your efforts toward a realization of such a future.

For tonight, God bless you all, may you achieve your heart's desire, and acknowledge with me that we are indeed all lucky we live in Hawai'i.

Thank you again for allowing me to share this occasion with you. *Me ke aloha pumehana.*

<u>Appendix</u>

Politics Hawaiian Style

Honolulu Star-Bulletin *Progress Edition, February 1989*

The first political campaign I remember was in 1932, the year that Franklin D. Roosevelt took the country solidly into the Democratic Party camp and left the Republican Party in shambles. In the Senate, Democrats outnumbered Republicans 59 to 36, and in the House of Representatives Democrats took 313 seats and Republicans took only 117.

Those were dog days for Republicans, but their fortunes declined even further. The 1936 presidential election produced the slogan: "As Maine goes, so goes Vermont." Those were the only states to vote Republican. And in the Congress, the Senate wound up with 75 Democrats to 17 Republicans, and the House of Representatives with 333 Democrats to 89 Republicans.

In Hawai'i in 1932, the most important elections were the races for county offices in the four counties. Our governor, secretary (as the lieutenant governor was then called) and judges were appointed by the president of the United States, a position held by Republicans from 1921 to 1933. In the county races, the Roosevelt coattails reached into Honolulu and elected five out of the seven supervisors. George Fred Wright survived to succeed himself as Republican mayor. The other two supervisors were Republicans Charles Crane and my father, Samuel Wilder King, in his first election.

From 1932 to 1952, elected Republicans in Hawai'i suffered a gradual attrition in numbers as Democrats were appointed by Presidents Roosevelt and Truman to be our governors, secretaries and judges, as labor unions committed to support Democrats gained in strength, and as our increasing urban population grew restless under the Neighbor-Island domination of the Legislature. The result of these and other forces was that our House of Representatives in 1947 consisted of exactly fifteen Democrats and fifteen Republicans. Republicans managed to come back, for a brief period, but the events of the 1950s put an end to what had been essentially fifty years of a Republican power structure.

During the period 1953 to 1955, Republicans were in control nationally and locally. Eisenhower was president, his appointee was governor, both houses of the Congress and both houses of our Legislature were controlled by Republicans, our delegate to Congress was a Republican. This golden opportunity for positive action for the benefit of Hawai'i was lost. Statehood for Hawai'i passed the House of Representatives, passed the Senate with amendments, and then died when it got back to the House of Representatives. The usually stated excuse was that Alaska had been tied to Hawai'i and for various reasons the president was opposed to statehood for Alaska. Yet, three years later, after Democrats had regained control of both houses of the Congress, President Eisenhower signed the bill making Alaska the forty-ninth state without Hawai'i. Hawai'i had to wait another three years when a Congress controlled by Democrats welcomed Hawai'i as the fiftieth state.

I was chairman of the Hawai'i Republican Central Committee in 1952-1953, and I well remember leading a delegation of local Republicans to a meeting with Vice President Nixon at the Royal Hawaiian Hotel. We expressed our opinion that, with Republicans in control at all necessary levels, there was every reason Hawai'i should get statehood, a Republican nominee for a judgeship of Japanese ancestry should be confirmed by the United States Senate and the Hawai'i Republican Party should be able to attract someone of national importance for its Lincoln Day dinner. We did not receive satisfaction on any of these modest proposals.

I believe that this failure on the part of the national Republican Party resulted in a loss of credibility for the local Republican Party on the part of the people of Hawai'i. This was an especially bitter pill for Republicans as the contributions of Republicans Samuel Wilder King and Joseph Rider Farrington were buried beneath the praise for Democrats John A. Burns and Lyndon Johnson. One was reminded of the story of the little red hen who had such difficulty getting anyone to help her bake bread but none at all in finding those who were willing to eat the finished project.

We are all familiar with the major role also played by our returning war heroes in taking over the Democratic Party under the leadership of John A. Burns. The combination of labor and young, energetic, well-educated and intelligent war veterans completed the process of shifting Hawai'i from a Republican territory to a Democratic state.

With statehood and its opportunity for total local control of our state and local governments, it seems to me that we have had continuous politics in every sense of the word. We had elections in 1958, 1959, 1960 and 1962 before we managed to get into phase with our normal schedule. We had regular and special sessions of our Legislature in 1959 and 1960. We voted for our original constitution twice, once when we proffered it to Congress and again after Congress made some amendments, and we have since had two constitutional conventions, both making substantial changes. We have created another electorate for the Office of Hawaiian Affairs. We have tinkered with county government with charter commissions, twice for Honolulu.

Some changes were imposed from without. Judge Martin Pence forced a revamping of the local Senate based on population, which resulted in a shift of control by the Neighbor Islands to control by Oʻahu. A three-judge federal court on which I sat forced a reapportionment of the Legislature, which resulted also in a redistricting of the City and County of Honolulu City Council. The past thirty years have also brought forth major legislative changes and experiments, the most important being undoubtedly the leasehold conversion law.

We are now entering a period of relative calm. The originally radical changes are accepted norms, or have passed into history or have been repealed. The only radical agenda today is provided by Hawaiian activists who seek greater self-government. Future elections promise to be held regularly every two, four or six years, depending on the office. The earlier hungry young Turks are for the most part now well-fed old nabobs. Streetwise candidates all run as Democrats, or switch to be Democrats after being elected as Republicans. Most of the exciting races are provided by Democrats running against Democrats.

Yet the interaction of many people in an advanced society will not allow a condition of calm to last very long. New forces are at work to bring about new changes. I have already mentioned Hawaiian activists. Another force, not entirely separate from the Hawaiian activists, is being forged by the graduates of our own law school. They have already achieved success in seeking elective office, including the office of governor.

We may expect our citizens of Filipino ancestry to become more of a force as their voting population grows, as it surely will. Naturalizations in Hawaiʻi's federal court are adding significant numbers of Filipino Americans every week. The impact of newcomers, especially from California, will, in my opinion, be greater in the future than it has been. Most of them come to Hawaiʻi conditioned to be Democrats, but as they bump up against an entrenched local power structure, they may be expected to react negatively to some of our established patterns of distributing jobs and opportunities.

The substantial Japanese investment in Hawaiʻi is bound to have an effect on our political future. Government and business are necessarily closely involved with each other. Neither can neglect the other without negative developments. Substantial business interests in the United States have always either sought to elect their own candidates or sought later accommodation with successful opposition candidates. There is no reason to believe that Japanese business moguls will act any differently.

Labor still dominates Hawai'i's politics, but here, too, there are signs of changes. Businesses continually, and successfully, seek ways to reduce their numbers of employees. Governments continually, and successfully, expand their numbers of employees. Today, the traditional working man's labor unions are overshadowed in political activity by the unions of government employees. This trend, in my opinion, will continue as traditional labor unions offer fewer opportunities to young people entering the labor market while government employment becomes more attractive.

Finally, a very numerous untapped potential political force exists among people connected with the military in Hawai'i who do not participate in local politics. Whoever develops a program that appeals to the self-interest of these people will have a source of new voters whose number could change the existing balance of political power.

All in all, I look forward to the next thirty years with an abiding trust in the collective wisdom of our people. A Chinese proverb that expresses my own belief states that three humble shoemakers are the equal of one great philosopher. ❧

Appendix

SAMUEL P. KING TIMELINE

1916	Born April 13 in Hankow, China
1922	Loses sight in left eye
1923-1928	Central Grammar School
1928-1933	Punahou School
1933	Finalist in National Oratorical Contest
1933-1937	Yale College
1937-1940	Yale Law School
1941	Assistant Attorney, Territorial Department of Public Works; Assistant Attorney, Territorial Department of Attorney General; on Oʻahu during December 7 bombing of Pearl Harbor
1942	Assistant Attorney, War Shipping Administration, Washington, D.C.
1942-1946	United States Navy, active duty
1943-1944	Navy Japanese Language School
1944	Married Anne van Patten Grilk in Boulder, Colorado
1945-1967	United States Naval Reserve
1946-1961	Private law practice in Honolulu

1947	Birth of Samuel Pailthorpe King, Jr.
1948	Birth of Louise van Patten Keali'iloma King
1950	Birth of Charlotte Lelepoki King
1953	President, Hawai'i Bar Association
1953-1955	Chairman, Hawai'i Republican Central Committee
1956-1961	Part-time O'ahu district magistrate
1961-1970	Circuit Court Judge
1965	Co-translator and co-editor with George Leckie of O. Korschelt's *The Theory and Practice of Go*
1966-1970	Co-founded Family Court with Judge Gerald Corbett
1970	Leaves bench; Republican candidate for governor
1971-1972	Member of Republican National Committee
1971	Represented Kamehameha Schools alumni and parents who questioned the Bishop Estate trustee selection process
1972-2010	U.S. District Court Judge
1974-1984	Chief Judge, U.S. District Court
1984-2010	Active calendar as Senior Judge
1997	Co-author of "Broken Trust" essay

2006   Co-author of the book *Broken Trust: Greed,*
                Mismanagement and Political Manipulation in
                America's Largest Charitable Trust

2010   Passes away on December 7 after accident
                at home

Family Tree

SAMUEL P. KING GENEALOGY

Keali'inohomalu
|
Kalaniho'oulumokuikekai
|
Mahi _____

William Heath Davis _____ Hannah Kalikolehua Holmes
|
Robert Grimes Davis _____

James Anderson King _____ Charlotte Holmes
| Lelepoki Davis
|
Samuel Wilder King
|

Anne van Patten Grilk _____

Samuel P. King, Jr. _____ Adrienne Caryl   Louise van Patten _____
| Sepaniak   Keali'iloma King |
| |
_____ |
| | |
Christopher Edward   Samuel Wilder _____ Tiffany |
Sepaniak King   King II   Herder |
                                                          _____
                                                          |
                              Juan Carlos _____ Anne Victoria
                              Fernandez Nieto   Leilehua Lanzilotti

Oliver Holmes

Charlotte Holmes ———————— Charles Hammett

Harriet Hammett

Kaniau

Thomas Evans ———————— Hana Kaniau

Pauline Nāwahineokalaʻi Evans

Samuel Pailthorpe King

Salvatore Samuel
Lanzilotti

Charlotte ———————— David Stretch
Lelepoki King

Sara Elizabeth Lelepoki
King Stretch

Charlotte Kathryn
Mahealani King Stretch

Leona Nāwahineokalaʻi
Lanzilotti

Index